Minute
Meditations™
on Prayer

BOB & EMILIE
BARNES

Minute
Meditations™
on Prayer

BOB & EMILIE
BARNES

HARVEST HOUSE™ PUBLISHERS

EUGENE, OREGON

Cover by Terry Dugan Design, Minneapolis, Minnesota

Harvest House Publishers, Inc. is the exclusive licensee of the trademark, MINUTE MEDITA-TIONS.

Every effort has been made to give proper credit for all stories, poems, and quotations. If for any reason proper credit has not been given, please notify the author or publisher and proper notation will be given on future printings.

MINUTE MEDITATIONS™ ON PRAYER
Copyright © 2003 by Bob and Emilie Barnes
Published by Harvest House Publishers
Eugene, Oregon 97402
www.harvesthousepublishers.com

Library of Congress Cataloging-in-Publication Data
    Barnes, Bob, 1933–
        Minute meditations on prayer / Bob and Emilie Barnes.
            p. cm.
        Includes bibliographical references
        ISBN 0-7369-1141-3 (pbk.)
        1. Prayer—Christianity—Meditations.   I. Barnes, Emilie.   II. Title.
        BV210.3.B37 2003
        248.3'2—dc21   2003002277

Printed in the United States of America

03   04   05   06   07   08   09   10   / BP-MS /   10   9   8   7   6   5   4   3   2   1

This book is dedicated to the thousands of prayer supporters we had during Emilie's illness. Without your steadfast petitions to God for healing, we would not be able to carry on our ministry as we have. At a very early time, our wonderful Dr. Barth stated that we needed a "divine intervention," and we have had one because of our wonderful prayer partners. Many days your cards, letters, and e-mails would arrive when Emilie needed that lift of encouragement. We have learned so much about prayer and its workings during this phase of our lives.

We thank God daily for a marvelous healing. Continue to pray for us because we still have many hurdles to jump. Thanks for your faithfulness.

Bob and Emilie Barnes

Contents

Introduction

One of the main purposes of faith is to bring us into direct, personal, and vital contact with God. When people pray, they are exhibiting an awareness of their helpless need and acknowledging that there is adequacy in prayer. Even though God knows all of our daily needs, our praying for them changes our attitude from complaints and criticism to praise. It permits us to participate in God's personal plan for our lives.

In Luke 18:1, Jesus was teaching His disciples through a parable to "show that at all times they ought to pray and not to lose heart." The disciples should not be discouraged because answers do not come immediately. Oh, how we have learned this through our fervent prayers for Emilie to be healed of her cancer and all that goes with being a cancer patient. We wanted immediate healing that would have the medical profession uttering, "It's a miracle!" but we've learned that God's timetable is much different than our own.

One of the great mysteries of prayer is why some are healed and not others. Why do some get miracles and others are left terminal? After endless months and years of petitioning to God, we have come to the realization that "God's will" will be done. He has a wonderful timetable for each of our lives. The sooner we recognize this in our Christian walk the quicker we will understand that His thoughts are greater than our thoughts and His ways are greater than our ways.

Yes, God healed Emilie of her mantle cell lymphoma, and we give praises to Him for that. From the very beginning we claimed John 11:4 as our theme verse: "This sickness is not to end in death, but for the glory of God, so that the Son of God may be glorified by it." What amazing peace we received when we turned this dramatic situation over to God and agreed with each other that through this valley, God was going to be glorified.

This declaration came about over years and years of previous prayers and the study of God's Word that proved we could trust God for everything—yes, even our lives. Through historical observation we knew God had our personal interest in His command. This kind of faith makes life so exciting. We don't have to search the world over for the purpose of life, we have found it and are living it daily. The Westminster Confession of Faith expresses it very clearly, "Man's chief end is to glorify God, and to enjoy Him forever." Prayer helps us establish this purpose of life for us. Without this we would have a holy god but no reason for why we are here on earth.

If we are to live meaningful lives we have the two options that Jesus gave His disciples in Luke 18:1: We are to pray and not lose heart. Around us are a Father's arms, and we are to cry out to Him because, in Jesus, His voice has already called out to us. We are to answer like children crying out to their father. Because, like children, we do not always know what is wrong with us.

When we face the many pressures of life, there is only one way out—we are to pray. Prayer is our way to the place of power; it is the way to certain solutions of our problems. Yes—it's an answer to all of our unbearable pressures. Prayer is crying out to our God we cannot see but whom we rely upon, a Father with a father's heart and a father's tender compassion and willingness to act. Prayer always stirs the heart of God. Prayer always moves God to act.

In the book of Romans, Paul reminds us that often we do not know what to pray for, but God knows. The Father knows because He is our father. He also knows when to answer in the particular way we asked and when it may not be the best thing to do under the circumstances.

The answer to a prayer request may indeed be long delayed, but there is no delay at all in an answer to the prayer itself. When we cry out there is immediately an answer—speedily God rushes to help. The answer may be the squeeze of the Father's hand on ours, the quiet comfort of the Father's voice, the reassurance of the Father's presence even though the stresses and pressures are still evident.

The purpose of prayer is to bring us into an understanding of the Father's heart. It brings us not always to the place of an answer, but to the place where a direct answer is unnecessary to an understanding of God's will for our lives. We cannot establish a relationship with God without communication. Human desires and needs require "speech." Prayer is an absolute necessity in the interchange of a believer's heart with the Father. Martin Luther once cried out, "O Father, teach us to pray."

In this book we center on the model prayer of Scripture: the Lord's Prayer. Even though many of us have prayed it since our earliest recollection, few have taken the time to break it apart and study the significance of each phrase. Although we created sections to follow the petitions of Matthew 6:9-13, we still invite you to skip around and choose the reading that seems most suited for the day ahead. At the top of each page you will see three boxes. Each time you read a meditation, put a check mark in one of the boxes so you can keep track of what you've studied.

Accompanying each devotion is a prayer to initiate your conversation with God. We also encourage the practical application of each day's message with a simple idea for action. You will find that during the day you will have transformed that one action idea into many—and the blessings just keep multiplying. To close each devotion, we added a bit of wisdom from Scripture or other sources of inspiration. Through all of these elements we pray you will discover a greater intimacy with the Giver of all wisdom—our Lord.

Many people choose to journal their prayers and reflections as a way to record their time spent with the Lord. You might consider this. Your entries could become a great testimony to God's faithfulness.

Let us begin by reflecting on the simple, well-known prayer found in Matthew. It opens with a compelling declaration of "Our Father who art in heaven," moves through six petitions, and ends with a mighty doxology and "amen." These powerful, memorable words serve as the guiding light for our devotional journey.

The Lord's Prayer

Our Father who art in heaven,
hallowed be Thy name.
Thy kingdom come.
Thy will be done,
on earth as it is in heaven.
Give us this day our daily bread.
And forgive us our debts,
as we also have forgiven our debtors.
And do not lead us into temptation,
but deliver us from evil.
[For Thine is the kingdom, and the power,
and the glory, for ever. Amen. (KJV)]

Matthew 6:9-13 RSV

Our Father Who Art in Heaven
Approaching His throne with reverence

This wonderful model of prayer begins with this adoration of God: *Our Father who art in heaven.*

God tenderly invites us to believe that He is truly our Father, and we are truly His children, so that we may ask of Him in all cheerfulness and confidence, as dear children ask of their dear father. James 4:2 states, "You do not have because you do not ask." As any loving Father, God wants us to boldly approach His throne and commit our requests, our adoration, our thanks, and supplications to Him in the form of prayer.

E.M. Bounds expressed it so simply when he wrote:

> God is always within call it is true; His ear is ever attentive to the cry of His child, but we can never get to know Him if we use the vehicle of prayer as we use the telephone—for a few words of hurried conversation. Intimacy requires development. We can never know God as it is our privilege to know Him by brief repetitions that are requests of personal favors and nothing more. That is not the way in which we can come into communication with heaven's King.

We try many ways to cope with the many stresses of life. Often we escape into work, leisure time, body toning, and exercise, and even many kinds of addictions. Often these escapes look like a way to survive, but behaviors turned to as responses to stress—even those with religious trappings—are not the solution. God Himself is the only one who can direct us to live life as He meant it to be.

Since God is so near to us, we can approach Him in a very personal way. When we open our prayer with the phrase "Our Father," we acknowledge that the answers of life lie beyond our abilities, our looks, our social position, and our economic status.

We admit that our might is not enough to live the fullest life that God intended for us. We have to be very brave to admit we need someone bigger than we are. But we can call upon the Father in confidence, knowing that we are His children and that He hears us.

We gain strength and confidence when we call on God by name and admit that we need Him for our every need and that we are helpless without Him.

No Busy Signals

Therefore, I want the men in every place to pray,
lifting up holy hands, without wrath and dissension.

—1 TIMOTHY 2:8

rayer is honored by our Lord, and we are commanded and told to have personal communion with Him. It is not something we have to do, but something we *get* to do. *What a privilege!* We need not make an appointment to get His attention. He is truly a 24/7 God; He is *always* available. Psalm 145:18 supports that principle: "The LORD is near to all who call upon Him." We aren't screened by an answering machine, caller ID, an administrative assistant, or a group of secretaries. Nope. God is always there for us. He never is too busy. He will never say, "Call back when My calendar isn't so full." We are invited to walk boldly into His presence at any moment, day or night.

Scripture tells us that we are known by Him. Just think, God knows our names. Truly, His invitation to prayer is a precious expression of His love for each one of us.

Here are a few verses of Scripture that might help us know about this wonderful opportunity to pray.

- ❧ "Seek the LORD and His strength; seek His face continually" (1 Chronicles 16:11).

- ❧ "...The prayer of the upright is His delight" (Proverbs 15:8).

❧ "At all times they [the disciples] ought to pray and not to lose heart" (Luke 18:1).

❧ "…The Spirit also helps our weakness; for we do not know how to pray as we should, but the Spirit Himself intercedes for us with groanings too deep for words" (Romans 8:26).

❧ "Be anxious for nothing, but in everything by prayer and supplication with thanksgiving let your requests be made known to God" (Philippians 4:6).

Prayer: *Father God, thank You for inviting me into Your presence. You are a God who is concerned about me. I love Your kindness and Your desire to hear my every need. Amen.*

Action: Choose one of the listed Scriptures to meditate on today. Thank the Lord for giving us a way to communicate with Him. Praise God for prayer.

Today's Wisdom: *"Jesus said to him, 'I am the way, and the truth, and the life; no one comes to the Father but through Me.'"*

—John 14:6

How Do I Pray?

*O Lord, hear me praying;
listen to my plea, O God my King,
for I will never pray to anyone but you.*

—PSALM 5:1 TLB

ave you ever thought, *What's the proper posture while I pray? Is it all right if I pray while I'm standing at the sink washing dishes? What about when I'm doing my other chores?* If I pray then, will God hear me as well as when I'm on my knees in a quiet room?

We've asked these questions. In searching for the answers in the Word of God, we discovered that all positions are appropriate for prayer. God gives great liberty to praying people. The important issue is that our hearts are in communion with Him as we pray. In Scripture, we discover many ways of praying:

- ❧ kneeling (1 Kings 8:54; Ezra 9:5; Daniel 6:10; Acts 20:36)

- ❧ standing (Jeremiah 18:20)

- ❧ sitting (2 Samuel 7:18)

- ❧ in bed (Psalm 63:6)

- ❧ in private (Matthew 6:6; Mark 1:35)

- ❧ with others (Psalm 35:18)

- ❧ hands lifted (1 Timothy 2:8)
- ❧ silently (1 Samuel 1:13)
- ❧ loudly (Acts 16:25)
- ❧ at all times (Luke 18:1)

Prayer: *Father God, as I fulfill my calling as a believer who loves You, please hear my every prayer—no matter what position I assume. Amen.*

Action: During the next week, try several different positions as you pray. Read the Scripture given that goes with each position.

Today's Wisdom: *"Prayer is neither black magic nor is it a form of a demand note. Prayer is a relationship. The act of praying is more analogous to clearing away the underbrush which shuts out a view than it is to begging in the street. There are many different kinds of prayer. Yet all prayer has one basic purpose. We pray not to get something, but to open up a two-way street between us and God, so that we and others may inwardly become something."*

—John Heuss

A Prayer Offered in Faith

*Is anyone among you sick? Let him call for the elders
of the church, and let them pray over him,
anointing him with oil in the name of the Lord.*

—JAMES 5:14

In this passage God may heal directly, through medicine, or in answer to prayer. The oil is a symbol of the presence of God (Psalm 23:5); it may also have been considered medicinal in James' day (Luke 10:34). Prayers of faith are answered not simply because they are prayed in faith but only if they are prayed in the will of God (1 John 5:14). God does not always think it best to heal. Paul had a thorn in the flesh which he prayed would be removed. However, the Lord said to Paul, "My grace is sufficient for you, for power is perfect in weakness." Paul replied, "Most gladly, therefore, I will rather boast about my weaknesses, that the power of Christ may dwell in me. Therefore I am well content with weaknesses, with insults, with distresses, with persecutions, with difficulties, for Christ's sake; for when I am weak, then I am strong" (2 Corinthians 12:8-10).

When I (Emilie) was first diagnosed with cancer, I went to the elders of the church and asked them to pray for me and anoint me with oil. It was a beautiful ceremony. I had never been anointed with oil before, thus I didn't know what to expect. However, I was desiring complete healing. When

I wasn't immediately healed I felt disappointed and was let down temporarily—not wanting to accept the fact that God said, "Not yet." It wasn't until many months later that I could see and feel the effects of my healing taking place.

Bob and I had come to agreement that we could and would be content with God's will in our lives. Even like Job when his wife told him to curse God and die, he replied, "Shall we indeed accept good from God and not accept adversity?" (Job 2:10).

Prayer: *Father God, I thank You for your provision, that we are to seek out the elders of our church and ask them to pray and anoint us with oil. It makes us depend upon Your will for us. Thank You! Amen.*

Action: Have great faith today as you lift up a prayer to God.

Today's Wisdom: *"If I am a Christian I am not set on saving my own skin, but on seeing that the salvation of God comes through me to others, and the great way is by intercession."*

—Oswald Chambers

Prayers That Produce

*The effective prayer of a righteous man can
accomplish much.*

—JAMES 5:16

*As I go to prayer each day,
Help me, Lord, to always stay
Fervent in the things I say;
You've done so much for me!*

—BRANON

Oh, how these words ring out to me. I (Emilie) can truly say that without the fervent prayers of those around this country who have earnestly prayed for me, I would not be alive today. Yes, the doctors, research staff, proper protocol, the pharmacists have had a great deal to do with my healing, but without the prayers of believers, I wouldn't be here. I thank all of my prayer supporters every day for their unending prayers.

Bishop Hall said many years ago,

> It is not the arithmetic of our prayers, how many they are; nor the rhetoric of our prayers, how eloquent they be; nor the geometry of our prayers, how long they be; nor the music of our prayers, how sweet our voice may be; nor the method of our prayers, how orderly they may be;

nor even the theology of our prayers, how good
the doctrine may be—which God cares for. Fervency of spirit is that which availeth much.

Prayer: *Father God, teach me to pray fervently. Let not
my words be mushy or weak, but let my petitions
and praise be dynamic in spirit. Help me to practice the art of prayer. May my words and actions
please You. Amen.*

Action: Pray fervently for another person today. Lift
up a friend, stranger, neighbor, or family
member and passionately pray to God on his
or her behalf.

*Today's
Wisdom:*   "He who has learned to pray has learned the
greatest secret of a holy and happy life."

                                    —William Law

Supported by God

Be still, and know that I am God.

—Psalm 46:10 KJV

While walking along the edge of the Dead Sea one day, a man lost his balance and tumbled into a deep section of water. Because he didn't know how to swim, he was panic-stricken. In desperation he began to thrash about, fearing he would drown. After a few minutes, he was completely exhausted and felt he could do no more. Crying out to God for help, he expected the worst. But what a surprise awaited him! As soon as he relaxed, he began to float. In his fear, he had forgotten that the Dead Sea is so full of salt and other minerals that if a person lies still, he will quickly come to the surface and float. All he needs to do is to trust himself to the buoyancy of the water.

This simple story was like us. Until we began to wait upon the Lord and to be still, we were treading water and getting hopelessly tired. Only then did we realize the safety that awaited us when we chose to be still, to rest in God. The eternal God is a never-failing help, but we must cast ourselves on Him and let Him sustain us.

Self-reliance is a trait we often strive to cultivate. We feel good when others notice how independent and self-sufficient we are. But the confidence and abilities we are blessed with should never become the barriers that keep us from immersing ourselves *completely* in God's love.

Prayer: Father God, let me stop striving and fretting and learn to rest completely in Your loving arms. Then I will find them more than adequate to support me in my time of need.

Action: Identify two things that keep you from immersing yourself completely in God's love. Write these down and pray over them.

Today's Wisdom: "In God's name, I beseech you, let prayer nourish your soul as your meals nourish your body. Let your fixed seasons of prayer keep you in God's presence through the day, and His presence frequently remembered though it be an ever-fresh spring of prayer."

—E.M. Bounds

Call to Me

Call to Me, and I will answer you,
and I will tell you great and mighty things,
which you do not know.

—JEREMIAH 33:3

od is good at all times, but He seems to be at His best when we are at our worst. In today's verse we are commanded to pray when it states, "Call to Me." Where was Jeremiah when God spoke to him? He was in prison!

Like Jeremiah, we are not merely counseled to pray—we are *commanded* to pray. When a hospital is built, it is considered sufficient that the doors are open to the sick when they need help. But no order is made that the sick must enter the hospital's care. So it comes as strange that when prayer is concerned, man needs a command to be merciful to his own soul. God issues an order of love without which the sons of Adam would rather starve than come and partake of the gospel feast. God's own people need a command to pray because we are subject to periods of worldliness, if, indeed, that is not our usual state. We give our strength and freshness to the ways of the world and our tiredness to the ways of God. Hence, it is that we need to be told to attend to that very act that should be our greatest happiness and our highest privilege to perform—to meet with our God. "Call to Me," He says, for He knows that we are apt to forget.

Prayer: Father God, may You never have to tell me to pray. I consider it a privilege to be able to converse with You daily—and many times more than just once a day. I appreciate You inviting me into Your presence to talk. Amen.

Action: Figure out when you are the most alert, aware, and energetic during the day. All this week, give 15 minutes of this time to God. Enjoy the lively dialogue!

Today's Wisdom: "Let it be your business every day, in the secrecy of the inner chamber, to meet the holy God. You will be repaid for the trouble it may cost you. The reward will be sure and rich."

—Andrew Murray

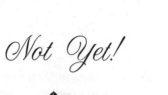

Not Yet!

Weeping may last for the night,
but a shout of joy comes in the morning.

—PSALM 30:5

God does not afflict or grieve the children of man for nothing. He shows this by the fact that He never allows affliction to last longer than there is a need for, and He never suffers them to be one moment longer in the furnace than is absolutely requisite to serve the purpose of His wisdom and love. Do not be discouraged when you suffer. He shall make your vineyard blossom and your field to yield its fruit. You shall again come forth with those who rejoice, and once more shall the song of gladness be on your lips. Hope yet, for there is hope. Trust still, for there are grounds for confidence. He shall bring you up from the land of your captivity, and you shall say of Him, "Thou hast turned for me my mourning into dancing" (Psalm 30:11 KJV).

In the book of Job, we read of Satan's tempting Job and afflicting him. But Job's circumstances changed and God restored him, "And the LORD turned the captivity of Job, when he prayed for his friends" (Job 42:10 KJV). Intercessory prayer was the sign of Job's returning greatness. It was the rainbow in the cloud, the dove bearing the olive branch, the voice of the turtle announcing the coming summer. When Job's soul began to expand itself in holy and loving prayer for his erring brethren, the heart of God showed itself to him by returning his prosperity and making him happy.

Prayer: *Father God, even in my peril You tell me "not yet." When I beg for relief You utter "not yet." I know all these sufferings are molding me into the person You want me to become. Help me keep my eyes on You for my deliverance. Amen.*

Action: Pray to be molded into the child of God you were born to become. During a time of personal struggle, look for opportunities to pray for others.

Today's Wisdom: *"Prayer does not mean simply to pour out one's heart. It means rather to find the way to God and speak with Him, whether the heart is full or empty. No man can do that by himself. For that he needs Jesus Christ."*

—Dietrich Bonhoeffer

Utter Prayer 14

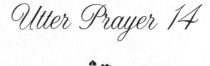

*"Seek My face," my heart said to You,
"Your face, O LORD, I shall seek."*

—PSALM 27:8

Prayer is as much a necessity of our spiritual life as breath is of our natural life. Have you been on your knees at times without the power to pray? Have you felt you could not petition as you desired? You wanted to pray, but your lips could not express what was in your heart?

There have been recent times when we had gone to God in earnest prayer so deep that we couldn't utter the same words again. We had previously petitioned God with the same words time and again. We didn't want to bother God with another request for healing for Emilie. Not only did we want healing of her lymphoma, but we wanted relief from her postherpetic neuralgia (nerve-ending damage due to prolonged shingles). These were biggy requests—we had prayed so often and seemingly with very little progress. At times we gave numbers to our prayers. Rather than repeating the same prayers over and over, we said to God, "We don't have the words to pray today; so we ask that you hear prayer 14."

Because we abide in Him and His words abide in us, He does hear our prayers even when they are a number. The Holy Spirit promises to intercede for us when we aren't able to pray for ourselves.

Prayer: Father God, thank You for hearing our numbered prayers. We don't seem to have the energy to go through the repetition of all the previous prayers we have uttered. Thank You for Your ear to hear our utterances. Amen.

Action: Create a list of prayers for your life. Memorize them and let your heart own them. Lift them up to the Lord, and He will hear your petitions.

Today's Wisdom: "Long my imprisoned spirit lay
Fast bound in sin and nature's night;
Thine eye diffused a quickening ray,—
I woke the dungeon flamed with light;
My chains fell off, my heart was free,
I rose, went forth, and followed Thee."

—Charles Wesley

Is Not This the Carpenter?

*Is not this the carpenter, the son of Mary, and brother
of James, and Joses and Judas and Simon?*

—MARK 6:3

Jesus was not accepted among the people of His hometown. They marveled at the crowds who gathered to hear the wisdom that came from His mouth. However, they were confused. "Is not this the carpenter?" They thought they knew Jesus too well; they couldn't believe that a simple carpenter could be elevated to the prominence where crowds would gather to hear Him teach.

One man who proclaimed Christ is remembered even today although he took a vow of poverty and lived a simple life. Saint Francis of Assisi died more than 775 years ago, but he has never been forgotten. Great men and women by the hundreds of thousands have lived and died—kings, conquerors, millionaires, artists, musicians, and scholars. All have been forgotten, but not Saint Francis of Assisi. The world stood back in wonder, for Saint Francis had no money, but he acted as if he were richer than the richest. This little man's body was scarred and wracked with pain, yet he sang sweeter than any bird. He was a beggar who smiled as he dined with the famous and laughed as he shared his last crust with a leper. He learned to love everything that lived as part of God's creation.

St. Francis had a secret worth knowing, and the world has been learning it from him ever since. The secret is the wisdom of Jesus, who some thought was just a carpenter. This plain carpenter was a builder of lives. He used more than lumber to create His structures. He used plain ordinary people just like you and me to further God's kingdom. Isn't that amazing?

As we are challenged to be like Jesus, may we, like Francis of Assisi, not let social status or societal limitations prevent us from becoming the person Christ wants us to become.

Prayer: *Father God, I, too, can be more than an ordinary carpenter. Light my path so I won't stumble along the way. Your light overcomes darkness and gives me hope for tomorrow. Help me share Your illumination. Amen.*

Action: Pray about your potential. Try to see yourself and your life through God's eyes. Ask God how He wants to use you. And be open to the answer!

Today's Wisdom: *"For it is God who works in you to will and to act according to his good purpose."*

—Philippians 2:13 NIV

☐ ☐ ☐

He Has, He Does, He Will

*Delight yourself in the LORD; and He will
give you the desires of your heart.*

—PSALM 37:4

May we always pray the prayer that is pleasing to the Lord and that would meet His approval. We know that God's will is going to be done. May we be willing to tell God that if our prayer is not proper or the best for us, to graciously deny our request. After long sessions of talking to God, we don't want anything that isn't in God's desire for our lives.

When we were a young married couple, we gave our children, our home, our marriage, and our possessions to the Lord—"take them and use them for Your glory." Now that we are older, we have given Him our lives even unto death. What a peaceful experience to give everything to Him. We don't have to worry about tomorrow because we know that it's in God's hand. We are reminded of three basic principles of prayer:

- ❧ God has
- ❧ God does
- ❧ God will

God has taken care of us in the past; He is taking care of us in the present; we can be assured that He will take care of us in the future. We always want to look back in time to remember what He has done for us. That awareness gives us great assurance that He can be trusted with our tomorrows.

Prayer: *Father God, our communion table has etched into its wood, "This Do in Remembrance of Me." May I never forget Your faithfulness in the past, and Your faithfulness in the present, so I can trust Your faithfulness for the future. Amen.*

Action: Remind yourself of times you have witnessed God's faithfulness. Share about these times with someone who needs to hear of His goodness.

Today's Wisdom: *"Glory in his holy name; let the hearts of those who seek the LORD rejoice."*

—1 Chronicles 16:10 NIV

Clear Out the Prayer Closet

And in the early morning, while it was still dark,
He arose and went out and departed to a lonely place,
and was praying there.

—MARK 1:35

harles Spurgeon once said, "Do not learn the language of prayer, but seek the spirit of prayer, and God almighty will bless you and make you more mighty in your supplications."

Every so often, we need to evaluate what's happening in our prayer lives. This way we can catch ourselves if we're slipping in our purpose and direction. Sometimes our prayers and methods become routine—not much is happening that's really meaningful. Maybe the hinges to your "prayer closet" door are rusty, but they do open and shut at their appointed times. Perhaps the doors are locked and cobwebbed. Or maybe you do not neglect prayer itself, but what a tale the walls might tell! "Oh!" the walls cry out. "We have heard you when you have been in such a rush that you could hardly spend two minutes with God. We have witnessed you coming and spending ten minutes and not asking for anything—at least your heart did not ask. The lips moved, but the heart was silent. We have heard you groan out of your soul, but we have seen you go away distrustful, not believing your prayer was heard, quoting the promise, but not thinking God would fulfill it."

We find ourselves going through the motions of prayer but not really praying. It's sort of like driving down the freeway at 65 miles per hour and not remembering the landscape that has whizzed by. We need to slow down and clear out the cobwebs from our minds as we kneel before God. He deserves our utmost awareness as we come before Him. Get excited about prayer time! Pay attention, be alert, stay awake.

Prayer: *Father God, may I go beyond the language of formal prayer, to seek the Spirit of prayer. May You bless me and honor my supplications. Amen.*

Action: Create a warm-up ritual before you pray. Prepare a prayer closet or choose a favorite chair, dim the lights, and curl up with a blanket as you speak to your heavenly Father.

Today's Wisdom: *"One night alone in prayer might make us new men, changed from poverty of soul to spiritual wealth, from trembling to triumphing."*

—Charles Spurgeon

Hallowed Be Thy Name
A petition of reverence to God's holy name

The first petition of the Lord's Prayer, *"Hallowed be Thy name,"* deals with the awesomeness of God's majestic name, which is given to no one else. The word "Thy" refers to God and His glory. In today's phrase, the concern is to look only to God and His glory. They echo our reverence and respect to Him.

No matter what our personal needs may be, we always honor our God first. The Lord's Prayer places man's needs and petitions *after* God is approached and glorified. Remember that when we pray even with the simplest of prayers we are in the presence of God and that He is there with us.

The word "hallowed" means to sanctify, revere, to make and keep holy. But why "be Thy name"? In the Old Testament the Jews would not use the name Jehovah when referring to their God, but would refer to God as "The Name." So here "Thy name" refers to all that God is in His majesty. "Thy name" literally means all that is true, all that has been revealed, all God's attributes, all that He has done, and all that He has ever done is to be greatly honored and revered.

Throughout Scripture we run across many various names that were associated to God:

> ❧ El or Elohim—which means His strength and power

> ❧ Jehovah—which means "the self-existent One," I Am that I Am

> ❧ Jehovah-jireh—The Lord will provide

> ❧ Jehovah-rapha—The Lord that healeth

> ❧ Jehovah-nissi—The Lord our Banner

> ❧ Jehovah-Shalom—The Lord our peace

ᴖ᭢ Jehovah-re-ah—The Lord our Shepherd

ᴖ᭢ Jehovah-tsidkenu—The Lord our Righteousness

ᴖ᭢ Jehovah-shammah—The Lord is present

These names of God reveal who He is—His character, His nature, His being, His attributes. When we enter into prayer, there is no way we can approach God as the "Big Daddy" or "The man upstairs." Our knees should tremble when we are in God's presence. We want the whole world to know what a privilege it is to go into prayer with God, whose name is above all names. He is great; He is mighty; He is majestic!

The name of God is indeed holy in itself; but we pray in this petition that it may be hallowed, or holy, also *among* us. We should so know God that our heart's desire should be that those around us and those throughout the world would come to know God as we do.

If we can honestly pray "hallowed be Thy name," then the rest of the prayer will fall into place. For the rest of the Lord's Prayer to be accomplished in our lives we have to hallow God's name.

Approaching the Throne of Grace

*Let us therefore draw near with confidence
to the throne of grace, that we may receive mercy
and may find grace to help in time of need.*

—HEBREWS 4:16

rue prayer is the drawing of my soul, by the grace of God, to the throne of God. It is not just the speaking of words or the emotions of my petitions that matter. He cares that I approach Him in day-to-day conversation. My style isn't as important as my desire to be in communion with Him.

There were times during Emilie's illness that we felt our utterances weren't going beyond the ceiling; however, from the promises of Scripture on prayer, and from God's answers of past prayers, we knelt assured that they had reached His ears. "But why, God, are You taking so long to get back to us?" we cried. After all, we sent it special delivery. Even though God didn't give us immediate answers, we were at peace knowing we would hear in His time frame and not by our watches. One thing we have learned is to have more patience, not only with God, but also with test results being delayed, with family and friends, and even with our smallest expectations.

Yes, we are to come with confidence to the throne of grace—where we obtain mercy and grace to help us in time of need.

Prayer: *Father God, we are not to be timid when we come into Your presence. May I be clear in my adoration of who you are, clear in my confessions, clear in my thanksgiving, and clear in my supplications. Thank You for being a hearer of my utterances. Amen.*

Action: Practice patience all day today: be patient with yourself once, others twice, and God at all times.

Today's Wisdom: *"And if we know that He hears us in whatever we ask, we know that we have the requests which we have asked from Him."*

—1 John 5:15

What Can I Do?

*I can do all things through Christ
which strengtheneth me.*

—Philippians 4:13 KJV

rammy, what is that verse of Scripture that says, 'I can do all things through Christ which gives me strength'?" "Oh, Chad, that's one of my favorite verses. Look up Philippians 4:13." The phone went silent for a few minutes and on comes my grandson Chad, who was about 12 years old at the time. I (Emilie) asked him why he wanted to know about that particular verse of Scripture. He replied, "Tomorrow I'm in a race for a presidential award at school, and I'm so nervous that I can't relax, and I needed that verse to give me added strength when I pray. Thanks, Grammy."

I told him I would pray for him tomorrow, and please call me back and let me know how he did.

Well, by 4:00 P.M. the next day the phone rang, and it was Chad on the other end. I knew by the excitement of his voice that he did well. I asked, "Chad, how did you do?" "Grammy, you won't believe it, but I won and set a new school record. I've never done so well. Thank you for your prayers and helping me find the verse."

That verse will be etched in Chad's memory. He will always be able to find that verse and will recall it whenever he needs extra strength. Yes, we can do all things through Christ who strengthens us.

Prayer: *Father God, You truly give me added strength by all Your promises. I'm so encouraged through Your Word. Amen.*

Action: Pray with the simple and unshakable faith of a child.

Today's Wisdom: *"The more helpless you are, the better you are fitted to pray, and the more answers to prayer you will experience."*

—O. Hallesby

Take Great and Little Things to Him

Let the children alone, and do not hinder
them from coming to Me.

—MATTHEW 19:14

hildlike confidence makes us pray as nothing else can. It causes a person to pray for great things they would never have asked for if they hadn't learned this simple assurance. We think that our great things are somehow worthy of God's attention, in reality our biggest petitions are little to God. In turn, we think our little things must be so small that it is not worth His time to bother with them. We need to realize that what is important to a child may be very small to his parent, and yet the parent measures the request, not from his own point of view but from the child's.

Have you ever heard your little child cry bitterly and you ran hurriedly to find out what was wrong? Upon examination, you discovered the cause of the pain was a small splinter in his finger. While you did not need to call a surgeon to take the splinter out, the injury was a great thing to your small youngster. Standing there with his eyes all wet with tears of pain, it never occurred to your son that his pain was too insignificant for you to care about. What are mothers and fathers made for but to look after the small concerns of their little children.

God, our Father, is a good father who pities us as human fathers pity their children. He counts the stars and calls them by name, yet He also hears and heals the brokenhearted and binds up our wounds. If you have put your confidence in God, you will take great concerns and little concerns to Him, knowing He will never disappoint your faith. He has said that those who trust Him "will not be put to shame or humiliated to all eternity" (Isaiah 45:17).

God always hears the prayers of a loving person because those prayers are the shadow of who He is.

Prayer: Father God, little or big, I bring my needs before You. If You number the sands on the beach, You are surely interested in the details of my life. Thank You for majoring on the minors of life. You are an awesome God. Amen.

Action: Cry out to God. Praise Him for the smallest and greatest of blessings. And cry for help in the midst of the smallest and greatest struggles.

Today's Wisdom: "Hear my prayer, O LORD, and give ear to my cry."

—Psalm 39:12

Be Content to Wait a Little

*Thou hast covered Thyself with a cloud so
that no prayer can pass through.*

—LAMENTATIONS 3:44

ait upon the Lord! We pray for patience and God
answers our prayers. We have learned to wait in
lines at the bank, at the check-out counter, at the
Department of Motor Vehicles, and at ball games. Wait, wait,
wait. All we get to do is wait. When it comes to answered
prayers, we don't want to wait. We want it in our time, not
God's time. We don't have a hundred years. Lord, now is the
appointed time.

Two of our all-time favorite friends have been George
and Ruth West (both are now home with the Lord). They
were much older than us at the time of our friendship. We
looked up to them as models of dignity. They were both tall
and very attractive. Ruth was our example of a truly femi-
nine lady—elegant in all areas of life. George was a Cary
Grant look-a-like. He was a very successful oil tycoon, and
often his vocabulary slipped and out came "roughneck language," to the embarrassment of Ruth. She would blush and
say, "Oh, George." Not until we got to know them did we
learn that Ruth had earnestly prayed for George's salvation
for 35 years. Here was a lady who was willing to wait for
God's timing. Later in life, George did come to know Jesus as
his Lord. What a day of celebration that was for all who

loved him. We always remember Ruth's faithful endurance when we lose patience with God and want an answer on our schedule. God's timing is always better than ours.

Don't let Satan discourage you by pointing out all of your unanswered prayers. We are dealing with a God whose day is like a thousand years and a thousand years is like a day. His timepiece is greater than a Rolex watch. Unanswered prayer doesn't mean He hasn't heard. In God's proper timing, He will give you an answer.

Prayer: *Father God, let me be still and wait upon Your timing for all my prayers. I know You have heard them because You say You have. Slow me down, and let my heart's desires be Your will in my life. Amen.*

Action: Call upon the name of the Lord for your every need. Be patient and know that He is Lord of all.

Today's Wisdom: *"God does not exist to answer our prayers, but by our prayers we come to discern the mind of God."*

—Oswald Chambers

Pray in Your Own Words

Be bold and strong! Banish fear and doubt!
For remember, the Lord your God
is with you wherever you go.

—JOSHUA 1:9 TLB

When you pray to God, tell Him what you want. If you do not have enough money, if you are in a tough strait, state the case—be specific in what you need. Speak in plain language; God needs no great oratories. Express your desires in the words you would normally use. They will be your best words. Name persons, name things, and take straight aim at the reason for your supplications.

One Friday night in Texas, I (Emilie) came down with such a fever and chills. I had to go to bed immediately when we came back to our guest suite provided by our wonderful hostess in her large Texas ranch home. We usually stay in a hotel, but this particular weekend we were provided these wonderful accommodations. We had been at church all day setting up for our Saturday organizational seminar. I was excited as always to share with women who were coming to hear how to be better wives, mothers, homemakers, and women of God.

But I was so sick! I knew that something had to change if I were going to be able to do a three-hour seminar before 500 women the next day. As I lay down on a soft feathery bed, I immediately fell asleep until past supper time. About 10:00 P.M. Bob came to bed. He woke me up to see how I was doing. I awoke in a drenching sweat, high fever, and shaking chills. At that moment Bob gave me a Tylenol and water. He held me in his big strong arms and prayed, "Lord, we come before You pleading that You will make Emilie well, and that You will give her an eight-hour window tomorrow so she can teach this group of women who have anxiously waited for this day. We thank You for hearing and answering our prayers. In Jesus' name we pray, amen."

Saturday morning I woke up like nothing had ever happened, ate breakfast, and conducted my sessions with the women. God did all that we requested, and we were so thankful. On the way back to the Dallas-Ft. Worth airport I began to feel bad again. Now, as I think back to the chills, fever, and sweats, I know they were the early warning signs of cancer. However, on this special weekend, the specific prayer uttered in a very simple language was heard and answered.

Prayer: *Father God, thanks for being a God who hears simple prayers. You have taught me that I need not be a great orator to get Your ear. You definitely give me the desires of my heart. Amen.*

Action: State the case. Ask. And know God is listening.

Today's Wisdom: *"Therefore we do not lose heart....For momentary, light affliction is producing for us an eternal weight of glory far beyond all comparison."*

                                            —2 Corinthians 4:16-17

Pray in All That You Do

*Give her the product of her hands, and let
her works praise her in the gates.*

—Proverbs 31:31

*L*ong before women entered the corporate world,
God provided them with a perfect model of a successful, godly woman who is an energetic, hard
worker.

We see her virtues by looking at the verses in Proverbs 31:

- ❧ She looks for wool and flax. She works with her
  hands in delight (verse 13).

- ❧ She is like a merchant ship. She brings her food
  from afar (14).

- ❧ She rises before sunup. She feeds her household
  (15).

- ❧ She considers real estate. She has her own money.
  She plants vineyards (16).

- ❧ She works out and is in good physical shape (17).

- ❧ She analyzes her profits. She plans ahead. She
  works into the night (18).

- ❧ She gives to those in need (19-20).

- ❧ She sews her household's garments (21).

❧ She sews to sell for a profit (24).

❧ She radiates good business practices (25-27).

❧ She attracts compliments from her family (28-29).

❧ She exudes excellence from her work and is praised in her neighborhood (31).

This woman knew all about work even though she didn't have an MBA from Harvard or Stanford. She was a woman who feared (respected) God, and because of her noble efforts in the workplace she was praised.

This attitude has a lot to say about modern man's approach to work. It's a far cry from the day when the adage was "To pray is to work, to work is to pray." In those days, work was a reflection of worship to God. People strived to serve and please the Lord through the work of their hands. It was the foundation for a strong work ethic. Oh, how it would do our souls good to return to this foundation and honor God in our work.

Prayer: *Father God, at times when I face the drudgeries of all that I have to do, when I wipe the sweat from my brow and my back aches from the weight of lifting, I forget that how I do my job is a reflection upon my worship of You. I truly want to wake up each morning with a song in my heart and an eagerness to start a new day. In the evening, before I fall asleep I want to praise You for another day's work. Let me be in continuous prayer while at work. Let me work for You and forget about the praises of man. Amen.*

Action: Let work be your prayer today. Let your every task be lifted up to honor God.

Today's
Wisdom:

"*It is our best work that He wants, not the dregs of our exhaustion. I think He must prefer quality to quantity.*"

—George MacDonald

Giving God the Time of Day

I will call on him as long as I live.

—PSALM 116:2 NIV

Have you ever really considered what God wants to give you during your daily time with Him? While you struggle to make time for God each day out of obedience…you may be missing God's purpose for this act.

God greatly *desires* to spend time alone with you. After all, you are His child (John 1:12; Galatians 3:26). He created you; He loves you; He gave His only Son for your salvation. Your heavenly Father wants to know you, and He wants you to know Him. God isn't asking you to go to the "time out" corner when you pray. He invites you into the palace of His heart. He invites you to know Him, rely on Him, and be blessed by Him.

If this time of solitude with God feels awkward or uncomfortable, begin by reading and meditating on God's principles or His Word for a while (using a devotional book like this one is a great start!), and then spend some time in prayer. Talk to God! Praise Him, thank Him, confess your sins, pray for your family and others, and pray for yourself.

Time with your heavenly Father is never wasted. If you spend time alone with God in the morning, you'll start your day refreshed and ready for whatever comes your way. If you spend time alone with Him in the evening, you'll go to sleep relaxed, resting in His care, and wake up ready for a new day to serve Him.

Remember, too, that you can talk to Him anytime, anywhere—in school, at work, on the freeway, at home—and about anything. You don't have to make an appointment to ask Him for something you need or to thank Him for something you have received from Him. God is interested in everything that happens to you.

Prayer: *Father, help me see the purpose of time spent with You. How I long to be in Your presence and feel Your love. I thank You for creating prayer and for caring about me enough to desire time with me. May I honor You by mirroring this desire and seeking out Your heart daily...not as an obligation, but as a privilege.*

Action: Consider your attitude toward time with the Lord. Do you see it as a privilege? If you do not, then spend time praying for insight about who God is. Get to know the Savior who desires time alone with you.

Today's Wisdom: "Trust in the LORD with all your heart, and do not lean on your own understanding."

—Proverbs 3:5

□ □ □

Praise Is Good and Pleasant

God is spirit, and those who worship Him must worship in spirit and truth.

—JOHN 4:24

The date September 11, 2001, will be a historic day in America's spiritual awakening. This was the day when, at 8:45 A.M. (EST) on a Tuesday morning, carefully planned acts of terrorism demolished the World Trade Center in New York, damaged the Pentagon in Washington D.C., and ended in decimation in rural Pennsylvania. Thousands of lives were lost.

In the days following, our country has experienced a great spiritual outpouring. Churches and synagogues have been overflowing with people who have wanted to praise God publicly. They have cried, prayed, sung songs, read Scripture, and heard pastors and teachers give messages on why evil exists in our world. Television and radio programs have been eager to cover these events throughout the world. United praise is good.

Psalm 150 reads:

> Praise the LORD! Praise God in His sanctuary, praise Him in His mighty expanse. Praise Him for His mighty deeds; praise Him according to

54

His excellent greatness. Praise Him with trumpet sound; praise Him with harp and lyre. Praise Him with timbrel and dancing; praise Him with stringed instruments and pipe. Praise Him with loud cymbals. Praise Him with resounding cymbals. Let everything that has breath praise the LORD. Praise the LORD!

Whereby single praise is good, united praise is like music in concert. There is nothing so pleasant to our ears, heart, and soul as to be a part of the body of Christ coming together in congregational praise. When I hear the joined voices of praise it makes me wonder what heaven will be like when all the angelic voices join together in great praise and worship.

There is something delightful in the union of true hearts in worship of God, especially when these hearts of praise are being expressed in song.

Prayer: *Father God, just to think about the united singing of praises to You gives me goosebumps. There is nothing so wonderful as to be a part of a chorus praising You in song. I look forward to every worship service at church when we as a body of believers lift our voices to praise You. Amen.*

Action: Join with another person today in prayer. Lift up the nation. Lift up the world.

Today's Wisdom: *"And you will seek Me and find Me, when you search for Me with all your heart."*

—Jeremiah 29:13

Prayers That Produce

Confess your faults one to another, and pray one for another, that ye may be healed. The effectual fervent prayer of a righteous man availeth much.

—JAMES 5:16 KJV

Throughout Scripture we are told to pray fervently. Jesus often stresses the power of fervent, believing prayer. In Matthew 7:7-11 we read of the abundant promises of grace that are fulfilled in the lives of those who intercede as they should. Verses 7-8 highlight fervency: "Ask and it will be given to you; seek and you will find; knock and the door will be opened to you. For everyone who asks receives; he who seeks finds; and to him who knocks the door will be opened" (NIV).

William Carey was once criticized because he spent so much time in prayer that he neglected his shoemaking business. But he believed that supplication, thanksgiving, and intercession were much more important than laying up treasures on earth. "Prayer is my necessary business!" he said. "Cobbling shoes is a sideline: it just helps me pay the expenses." The Lord honored Carey's vigorous faith, and he later became a well-known missionary to India.

The Scriptures mention several "effectual, fervent" prayers that were answered. Check out Joshua 10:12-13; 2 Kings 4:32-35; Isaiah 37:21, 36; Acts 16:23-26. Each of us can have a stronger, more effective prayer life. Commit to spending more time in prayer daily.

Prayer: *Father God, teach me how to have a more fervent prayer life. Bring alongside a mentor who can show me how to be more effective in my quiet time. Amen.*

Action: Pray today—and mean it!

Today's Wisdom: "When thou feelest thyself most indisposed to prayer yield not to it, but strive and endeavor to pray even when thou thinkest thou canst not pray."

—Hildersam

A Day Filled with Prayer

*Be joyful in hope, patient
in affliction, faithful in prayer.*

—ROMANS 12:12 NIV

Prayer is so important in our daily lives. Start each day with a prayer of thanksgiving for a new day, and end each evening with a prayer of thanksgiving for the provisions of the day.

As we spend time with God, we open ourselves to His work in our hearts and in our lives. Then, as we see Him working, we will want to know Him even more. We will want our prayer life to be all that it can be. What does that mean? How should we be praying?

As meaningful as the Lord's Prayer is to us, we have also found Colossians 1:9-12 to be a powerful guide in our prayer life:

> For this reason also, since the day we heard of it, we have not ceased to pray for you and to ask that you may be filled with the knowledge of His will in all spiritual wisdom and understanding, so that you may walk in a manner worthy of the Lord, to please Him in all respects, bearing fruit in every good work and increasing in the knowledge of God; strengthened with all power, according to His glorious might, for the attaining of all steadfastness and patience; joyously giving

thanks to the Father, who has qualified us to share
in the inheritance of the saints in light.

Think about how wonderful a prayer this is for you to
pray for your mate and your friends!

We also encourage you to tell your friends that you are
praying for them each day. If they are receptive, tell them the
specifics of your prayer for them. Let us assure you that it is
a real comfort to have friends praying for you, asking God to
give you wisdom and understanding, to enable you to honor
Him in all you do, to help you bear fruit for His kingdom,
and to grant you strength, steadfastness, and patience.

Know, too, that these verses from Colossians are a good
model for your prayers for other members of your family,
your neighbors, and yourself. All of God's people need to
know His will, to honor Him in everything they do, to grow
in the knowledge of the Lord, and to be steadfast as they
serve Him.

Prayer: *Help me, Lord, to be spiritually wise and to pray*
for the people around me. Amen.

Action: Make a weekly list of family members to pray
for. Each day of the week pray for a different
person.

Today's
Wisdom: *"Draw near to God and He will draw near to*
you."

—James 4:8

Obey My Commandments

I will wash mine hands in innocency:
so will I compass thine altar.

—PSALM 26:6 KJV

f unbelievers or even disobedient children of God had the promise put into their hands that reads, "Whatsoever ye shall ask in prayer, believing, ye shall receive"—they would be sure to ask for something that would support them in their unbelief or disobedience. But as is the person, such will be his prayers. God doesn't honor the requests of people asking for things that would support or encourage their own waywardness.

It is true that if we keep His commandments He will answer our prayers according to His will. If we reject God, He will not answer our prayers until we repent. Leviticus 26:21,24 KJV reads, "If ye walk contrary unto me...will I also walk contrary unto you." We will never have perfect innocency, but we can have an innocence of not wanting to sin and rebel from God. We need to approach God with honesty and reverence.

Praying with a heart of obedience and with a spirit of submission blesses a life with the joy of walking with God and in His will. It is so amazing to lift up petitions and desires and know they are heard, know that you will not be rejected, and know you are safe in the grip of God's will for your life.

Prayer: Father God, as I wash my hands with soap and water may it be a reminder to me to clean my heart, soul, and mind. I cherish the idea to be innocent before You. Forgive me of the past, and refresh me for the future. Help me to truly believe in my salvation and renewal in Your perfect grace. Let my life reflect this understanding. Amen.

Action: Submit to God's will. Search your heart for something you have been holding on to and release it to God.

Today's Wisdom: "For by grace you have been saved through faith, and that not of yourselves; it is the gift of God."

—Ephesians 2:8 NKJV

Thy Kingdom Come

*A petition for the quick establishment
of God's kingdom on earth*

This second petition in the Lord's Prayer emphasizes the importance of honoring the status and position of God.

The heart cry of all Christians is to have God establish His kingdom on earth. As we look at our world situation and view the evening news, we, as believers, yearn for the peace and tranquility God offers. It is very evident that Satan has his rule over the earth. Why should we be surprised when we observe the downward slide of America and the rest of the world. Satan's kingdom is running its course in history. Those of us with clarity of vision can easily see the results that this kingdom of darkness bestows on mankind.

The tension that exists in the present world affairs is that we as believers want to see God's name glorified, but Satan and his army put up strong opposition to such. The god of this world, the god of darkness, of evil, of deceit, is opposed to our God and His glory and honor.

But don't be discouraged! Throughout Scripture and history God has revealed that He is going to establish His kingdom in this world! God is going to assert Himself and take possession of this world that He created. Someday it will all be His glorious kingdom. In the meantime, we are to prepare for His return.

John the Baptist preached, "Repent ye: for the kingdom of God is at hand" (Matthew 3:2 KJV). This petition is as true today as it was in the day of Jesus' ministry. We are to look forward to the day when God will again establish His kingdom on earth.

We as believers need to have the blessings of His return in our hearts each day. Our radiance should glow to the world, showing we have eternal hope that God will conquer the wickedness of the world. We are to be the salt and light of the world. Others need to see Christ reflected in our everyday lifestyles.

In Revelation 22:20 we read, "Yes, I am coming quickly." Believers reply, "Amen. Come, Lord Jesus"!

With this assurance we can live in peace. We don't have to know what comes next. We don't have to be anxious for tomorrow because we know who brings tomorrow. We don't have to plan what to do if this or that happens since we can continually look upward and recognize that God has it all under control. His kingdom will return!

Approaching the Throne in Prayer

Thus says the LORD, "Heaven is My throne. . . ."

—ISAIAH 66:1

eal prayer is more than just a few words uttered in despair. Preparing ourselves spiritually before we begin our utterances upward can help us focus on the Lord. Yes, God does hear the prayers from those who seek salvation without first preparing themselves spiritually. There first must be a need and an awareness that they need God to cleanse them from their sins. But for those who are believers it's good to find a quiet place physically and mentally as we approach the throne of God with reverence. Isn't it wonderful to go directly to God through Jesus and the Holy Spirit? Through them we have immediate access. Our "prayer closet" has given us an opportunity to prepare ourselves spiritually before we try to approach the throne through prayer.

We can't shoot from the hip, hoping to hit God in the ear. Our words, to be effective, must be insulated with God's grace. After all, the only way we go directly to God and His radiance is through the filtering of the Holy Spirit.

When there is a real crisis in our lives, we are easily thrown to the cross. Our hearts are so tender that we are easily in the proper attitude for earnest prayer. Times of suffering prepare our hearts to be right with God. We are no longer puffed up or have false securities. We have finally realized and experienced the true realities of life. We know that we are lesser creatures than God. His true position in our life has been fully realized. He is the potter, and we are His clay. He will mold us in His own way.

Prayer: *Father God, I don't want to barge into the throne room as a rude guest. I want to prepare my heart spiritually before I come to You. Give me time to adore, confess, and give thanks before I present my supplications. Amen.*

Action: Prepare your heart to be in the presence of the Lord. Reflect on a favorite verse.

Today's Wisdom: *"Surely goodness and lovingkindness will follow me all the days of my life, and I will dwell in the house of the LORD forever."*

                                                   —Psalm 23:6

Your Household God

*Prayer is talking with God and telling Him you love
Him, conversing with God about all the things that
are important in life, both large and small,
and being assured that He is listening.*

—C. NEIL STRAIT

*I*s it okay to pray for worldly matters?" Philippians
4:6 reads, "In everything by prayer and supplication with thanksgiving let your requests be made
known to God." Prayer is not merely for spiritual matters,
but it's also for everyday concerns. We may take our smallest
requests directly to God. He is truly our "household" God.

We all have been around eloquent people who pray with
all the right words, great inflection of voice, and with enough
power to not need a microphone. Their prayers are so powerful that they are intimidating, and you don't want to
follow that person in prayer. We would much rather hear a
prayer that is humble in nature and one that encourages us:
"O Lord, I feel myself such a sinner that I can scarcely speak
to You. Please help me to pray! O Lord, save my poor soul!
Oh, that you would save my old friends! Lord, bless our
pastor. Be pleased to give us a revival. I can say no more.
Hear me for Jesus' sake! Amen."

Wow, when I hear a person pray like this, I can truly get
behind that person. I know he means every single word. I
don't want him to stop. His elementary style of worship

through prayer truly lifts me closer to God. I am compelled to pray when he finishes his conversation through prayer.

God truly wants us to pray about the simple things of life. He is a God of the household as well as the God of the heavens. We should be specific in identifying all that we want to mention before God. We can pray for our family members, our neighbors, our church staff, our missionaries, our relatives, and our government officials. God is concerned about the smallest of our desires. Visualize that God is instantly in the process of answering these household requests. A well-worded, 3-minute prayer is more effective than a 30-minute prayer with all of its eloquence.

Prayer: *Father God, let my prayers be compared with simple and clear words. Let not my speech be confusing and complicated. I want my prayers to be for those around me and my household. Amen.*

Action: Pray about something you have held back on. Something simple. Or small. Or basic. God welcomes this prayer.

Today's Wisdom: "Until a man has found God and been found by God, he begins at no beginning, he works to no end. He may have his friendships, his partial loyalties, his scraps of honor. But all these things fall into place, and life falls into place, only with God."

—H.G. Wells

A Heart of Love

*And I will give you a new heart—I will give you
new and right desires—and put a new spirit
within you. I will take out your stony hearts of sin
and give you new hearts of love.*

—EZEKIEL 36:26 TLB

As you begin to meet with God and spend time with Him regularly, you will realize your old heart can't make you a godly person. You try by making adjustments here and there and trying to fix a few shortcomings. But soon the realization hits—you can't make that transformation happen under your own power—fortunately, as a Christian, you don't have to!

Thankfully, not every one of us will need a new physical heart, but each of us does need a new spiritual heart. Why? Because we are born with a sinful nature.

What are we to do? Not even the most skilled physician can cure a sinful heart or give us a new pure one. But God can, and according to His promise, He will.

This heart surgery is performed by the loving hands of your Divine Physician. It doesn't require medical insurance. There are no disclaimers or deductibles. God offers this transformation to us free of charge. It cost Him greatly—His only Son died for our salvation—but it's a gift to us. All we have to do is accept it.

Prayer: *Father God, we all need a new heart—one that You alone can give. Thank You for performing spiritual surgery in my life. May I be thankful for this gift. The beating of this new heart will become the power of my life. Amen.*

Action: In your journal, write down five areas of your life where you would like a change of heart. Pray over these areas each day for a month and record the transformations.

Today's Wisdom: *"God grant me the serenity to accept the things I cannot change; courage to change the things I can; and wisdom to know the difference."*

—The Serenity Prayer

What Shall I Do with Jesus?

*Pilate said to them, "Then what shall I do
with Jesus who is called Christ?"*

—MATTHEW 27:22

hen I (Emilie) was a young girl, I anxiously
waited each week for one of my favorite television shows, "The $64,000 Question." A contes-
tant would answer all kinds of questions in a multitude of
categories. If he or she was successful over a period of
weeks, the person could arrive to the plateau of answering a
series of questions that, if answered correctly, would award
them $64,000.

I couldn't imagine that much money or that anyone
could be smart enough to answer those very difficult questions. To my disappointment, a scandal broke that charged
the producer of the show with leaking answers to the con-
testants so they could continue up the scale and build excitement for the TV viewers. I was disheartened because I
believed that someone was smart enough to answer all the
questions of life with surety.

It wasn't until I was dating my Bob that I would be con-
fronted with the most basic, fundamental, and important
question in my life. After coming home one evening from a
wonderful date, we were sitting on the sofa of my living

room apartment when he asked me the same question that Pilate asked the crowd in today's Scripture reading: "What shall I do with Jesus who is called Christ?" I had never in my young life been asked that question. I had been raised in a Jewish family and had recently graduated from Hebrew school; Jesus wasn't a name to be discussed in my circle of family and friends.

I asked Bob, "What do you mean? Why do I need to answer that question? I'm a good Jewish girl, I'm not a sinner, and I have no need for Him. I believe in God."

I knew that Bob was a Christian and believed differently than I did, but what did Jesus have to do with it? In the quietness of that room, Bob began to share with me who this Jesus was. He gave me the full gospel of the birth, the life, and the resurrection of this man named Jesus. He very lovingly shared the plan of salvation with me and told me that he would pray for me regarding the answer to the big question he had asked. In the weeks and months that followed, Bob asked my mother if he could take me to church with him. My sweet and darling mother said yes. I couldn't believe she would give me permission to go to a Christian church.

While attending the services, I heard teaching from Scripture that really made me ask questions—questions I had never thought about before.

Then one night in the stillness of my bedroom I knew how to answer Bob's question, "What shall I do with Jesus who is called Christ?" At that instant I asked Jesus to come into my life, to forgive me of my sins, to become my Lord and my Messiah.

The rewards that evening were worth far more than the $64,000 offered on my favorite TV show.

Over the years I have realized that this is the greatest question any person must answer in life. How you answer that question will determine what road your life will take.

How do you answer that question?

Prayer: *Father God, as I look back over the years, I'm so glad I answered that question with a big "yes" when I was a young Jewish girl of 16 years old. That became the foundation for all the other questions to follow in my life. Daily I appreciate what Jesus did on the cross for me. Amen.*[1]

Action: Ask yourself the most important question of all, "What shall I do with Jesus who is called Christ?"

Today's Wisdom: *"I'm going to heaven, and I believe I'm going by the blood of Christ. That's not popular preaching, but I'll tell you it's all the way through the Bible. I may be the last fellow on earth who preaches it, but I'm going to preach it because it's the only way we're going to get there."*

—Billy Graham

Nothing But Jesus

*For ye are dead, and your life is hid
with Christ in God.*

—Colossians 3:3 kjv

We have learned in life that if we move away from Jesus we're like the pruned grapevine that is cast on a pile to be destroyed. There is a delicate balance between the branch and the vine. In order for the branch to sprout new growth and produce grapes, the branches need to be pruned properly. When God is pruning us, He wants us to grow vines that produce new fruit. When we go out to the rose bushes and cut them back, we know we're not going to like what we see, but come spring we're so glad that the pruning shears removed all those dead branches. Now there is lovely vegetation growing where the roses have new wood to bloom.

If we are to have power in our prayers and our Christian walk, we must be sure that we stay close to Jesus even when the pruning shears are cutting all the branches away in our lives. When we are in the midst of being pruned we often ask, "Where is Jesus when I need Him?" These are the times when we really need to cling close to Him.

We are all created to worship something. The media projects all kinds of alternatives to satisfy our worship hunger. For some it means turning to a small god—like sports, wealth, fame, a job; for others we choose a big God—like the

Trinity: the Father, the Son, and the Holy Spirit. We must be careful in choosing whom we will serve. We must ask, "What is the object of our faith?" If it is anything or anyone other than Jesus, we must cut away all that binds us to that false god and return back to our first love—Jesus.

Satan is prowling like a lion trying to devour those who are careless in their faith. So we need to know to whom we belong. Continue to experience the joy and the peace of fellowship with God. We should let the faith of our union with Jesus remain in us forever. Jesus is all we need!

Be on guard that Satan doesn't try to seduce you away from the Lord. Continue to abide in Jesus' holy name.

Prayer: *Father God, Joshua's declaration, "for me and my house, we will serve God," is my battle cry. Even in the midst of pruning, I choose to serve God, my Creator. Amen.*

Action: Exchange your hunger for earthly things into a longing for God's heart.

Today's Wisdom: *"If we wish to pray with confidence and gladness then the words of Holy Scripture will have to be the solid basis of our prayer. For here we know that Jesus Christ, the Word of God, teaches us to pray. The words which come from God become, then, the steps on which we find our way to God."*

—Dietrich Bonhoeffer

Seek His Face

*So I gave my attention to the Lord God
to seek Him by prayer and supplications....*

—DANIEL 9:3

od will hear the prayers of those who give attention to the Lord. The lukewarm person gets
nowhere in the race of life. The warriors who win
the battles are those who are resolved to conquer or die.
People who are successful in this world are those who do
their business with passion and enthusiasm. When are you
most passionate? What triggers heartfelt devotion in your
everyday life?

My (Bob) mother used to remind us boys Saturday
morning as we began our chores, "Boys, if it's worth doing,
it's worth doing well." In essence, she was teaching us that
we are to give 100-percent effort to do the very best job we
could do. We also knew that at the end of the day our father
would come around and inspect our work. Nothing was
worse than having to redo a job. We had to pay attention to
our father in order to hear what he was telling us.

Have you ever experienced the frustration of doing
something halfheartedly and then having to go back and
repeat the action? All along it would have been easier to
pursue the task or responsibility with initial commitment
and purpose. We make things harder on ourselves when we

do not back our work, actions, and prayers with 100-percent effort and devotion.

That's the way we are challenged today. Pay attention and seek God's face. We must establish the proper priority for our relationship to our Lord before we go to Him with our petitions and supplications.

Prayer: *Father God, let me be awake as I come to You with my prayers. I want to look You eye to eye. No looking away, no laziness, no wandering— nothing to distract me from paying attention to You. Amen.*

Action: Have you made God a priority? Discover a passion for God through prayer. Make it a priority to enter His presence deliberately and purposefully.

Today's Wisdom: *"And whatsoever ye shall ask in my name, that will I do, that the Father may be glorified in the Son."*

—John 14:13 KJV

Strike the Same Note

*But seek first His kingdom and His righteousness;
and all these things shall be added to you.*

—MATTHEW 6:33

f we as believers dwell with God and God lives in
us, we will desire what God desires for us. We will
not deliberately ask for something that would not
be pleasing to God. Charles Spurgeon usually added at the
end of his prayers,

> Lord, if I have asked for anything that is not
> according to your mind, I ask you to disregard it.
> And if any wish that I have expressed to you—
> even though it is the desire that burns in my
> bosom above all other wishes—is a wish that is
> not right in Your sight, disregard it, my Father.
> But in Your infinite love and compassion, do
> something better for Your servant than Your ser-
> vant knows how to ask.

What a wonderful addendum to all our prayers!

Have you ever realized partway through a difficult conversation or meeting that you are not "on the same page" as
your spouse, friend, or coworker? It is like the light bulb
going on over a cartoon character's head. You suddenly
understand that the two of you are seeking two different
goals or outcomes. You do not share a vision for what you

are striving for. It is the same with our relationship with God.

If we could so humbly approach the throne of God that our thoughts are open to His, we would be surprised to see how our prayers fall into line with God's will for our lives. This would be for all our petitions—sickness, death, life, children, jobs, relationships, marriage, business dealings, purchases, and so on. All supplications would fall under the shadow of this umbrella.

Prayer: *Father God, I don't want any of my prayers to be different than what You know is best for me. May I be humble in petitioning my heart's desires—I truly don't want them if they would not be good for me. I want my prayer to be Your will. Amen.*

Action: Think about what "seeking His kingdom" means in your life. Get on the same page with the Lord by studying His Word and nourishing your life with His wisdom.

Today's Wisdom: *"Teach me to do Thy will, for Thou art my God; let Thy good Spirit lead me on level ground."*

—Psalm 143:10

The Humble Shall Hear

And David was dancing before the LORD
with all his might.

—2 SAMUEL 6:14

Wy hen we have answered prayer, we should always follow it with praise. When the Lord has been gracious to our prayers, we should praise Him! Don't be silent; those around you need to hear of God's grace to you. As I (Emilie) have had so many of my prayers answered, I want to be the first to thank God in public for all He's done. My favorite Scripture during this dark period of my life has been John 11:4 which reads, "This sickness is not unto death, but for the glory of God, that the Son of God may be glorified by it."

Praise is a healthy exercise; it is the most heavenly of our Christian duties. When we praise God for answered prayers, we benefit our fellow believers: "The humble shall hear thereof, and be glad" (Psalm 34:2 KJV).

Don't be a silent Christian—be willing to sing and give praises to God.

The great doxology of the church written by Thomas Ken and attributed to Louis Bourgeois, a German Psalter, took these words—

> Praise God, from whom all blessings flow,
> Praise Him all creatures here below,

Praise Him above ye heavenly host,
Praise Father, Son, and Holy Ghost. Amen.

—and made them ring out each Sunday in many of our churches. These words recognize that as the creatures of God's creation we are to praise our magnificent God. In Psalm 109:30 we read, "With my mouth I will give thanks abundantly to the LORD; and in the midst of many I will praise Him."

We are to be in a state of continuous praise to God for what He has done in our lives. He is everything to us: our healer, our provider, our comforter, our Savior, our redeemer, our security.

Prayer: *Father God, I am encouraged when I hear from others how gracious You have been in their lives. May all of us stand and be noted as ones who are thankful. Help us to not let bashfulness stop us from sharing. Amen.*

Action: Think about when you are silent about God's activity in your life. Look for a chance this week to speak out about God's goodness.

Today's Wisdom: *"Sometimes we must wait for God to do as we ask because the answer involves changes in other people, or even ourselves, and that kind of change always takes time."*

—Dallas Willard

The Power of Prayer

All Scripture is inspired by God
and profitable for teaching,
for reproof, for correction,
for training in righteousness.

—2 TIMOTHY 3:16

o you believe in the power of prayer? Many Christians do not. They think prayer is a good thing, but they do not think it is always successful. They figure that prayer's effect depends upon many other things, but that it has no power by itself.

Emilie's oncologist says that his patients with faith do much better than those who have no faith. Many times he calls for "divine intervention" to help with his medical solutions. Prayer is one of the most powerful change agents in the universe. When a person prays, it isn't a matter of whether God will hear him or not; God must hear him—because He promises that He will. First John 5:14 reads, "And this is the confidence which we have before Him, that, if we ask anything according to His will, He hears us." God has promised to hear our prayers, and He will not go against His promise.

In church history, the great pillars of the church had one thing in common—great prayer lives. And we have never read about or met a notable Christian known for his or her journey and contributions in life that was not also known for powerfully exercising prayer. When Charles Spurgeon had people visit his large church in London, England, during the latter part of the nineteenth century, they would ask him, "What is the success of this church?" Charles would lead them down a flight of stairs to the basement and show them a group of people on their knees praying for the ministry of the Metropolitan Tabernacle. They were a 24/7 praying church. They knew that if there wasn't continued prayer being given, the ministry would have no power.

We all should be challenged to have a powerful prayer life. Through people who pray God will honor ourselves, our families, our churches, and our ministries. Yes, there is power in prayer!

Prayer: *Father God, history has demonstrated that great things are accomplished through great prayer time. Help us exercise the privilege that we have in meeting with You daily. Amen.*

Action: Schedule and commit to spending one full hour in prayer this week.

Today's Wisdom: *"In every care it is the love which was fulfilled in the cross of Christ. It is the love of Jesus Christ himself, who went patiently and obediently to the cross—it is in fact the cross itself. The cross is the differential of the Christian religion, the power which enables the Christian to transcend the world and to win the victory."*

—Dietrich Bonhoeffer

Never Stop Praying

Pray without ceasing.

—1 Thessalonians 5:17

Throughout Scripture we are urged to "call upon the Lord" when we are sick, unable to provide for our families, or when our griefs overwhelm us. We are told to pray without ceasing for we have plenty of reasons to continually be in the Spirit.

As I (Emilie) lay in a bed at the cancer clinic getting treatment and as I searched Scripture, I began to ponder this thought of looking up verses regarding prayer. Ever since my early Christian experience I have heard about prayer, but to be honest with you, I never really understood it. I knew I was to pray, but I wasn't sure how it worked in one's life. Here are a few passages that are meaningful to me today:

- Call upon Me in the day of trouble; I shall rescue you (Psalm 50:15).

- Pour out your heart before Him (Psalm 62:8).

- Seek the LORD while He may be found; call upon Him while He is near (Isaiah 55:6).

- Ask, and it shall be given to you; seek, and you shall find; knock, and it shall be opened to you (Matthew 7:7).

❧ Draw near to God and He will draw near to you (James 4:8).

❧ Devote yourselves to prayer (Colossians 4:2).

With all of these promises we never need to ask, "May I be permitted to come into Your presence?" God desires communication. And to experience the abundance of God we only need to ask. Your Father in heaven is waiting to give you good gifts.

Prayer: *Father God, prayer seems like an all-day affair for me. Prayer needs flash before my eyes constantly. Thanks for being there when I need to talk to You. Amen.*

Action: Reread the prayer-affirming Scriptures and dwell on them. Let each verse teach you about conversing with God. Apply this wisdom to your day.

Today's Wisdom: *"And this is the confidence which we have before Him, that, if we ask anything according to His will, He hears us."*

—1 John 5:14

Be in Love with Prayer

When I awake, I am still with Thee.

—PSALM 139:18

Isn't it great to know that even though we sleep eight to ten hours, when we awake God is still with us? He hasn't dozed off during the early hours of the morning. We know that when we are the closest to Jesus, our prayers come easier and more often. During dry seasons of life we have to consciously set a time for prayer—and often it's more out of duty than desire. As we abide with our Savior, we don't have to say, "It is time for us to get to our task and pray." No, we pray when there is a need, regardless of the time of day or night.

These last few years have brought us to God's throne because we want to, not because we fall back to the law. If you aren't there yet, just wait. The sufferings of life will cause you to drop to your knees in earnest prayer.

In our earlier Christian walks it was hard to understand the meaning behind 1 Thessalonians 5:17, where it states, "pray without ceasing." Now we have experienced that in real, living color. We pray literally without ceasing. We pray when we wake, pray at meal time, pray throughout the day, and we end our day with a prayer of thanksgiving for getting us through the day.

When a friend calls to tell you of a prayer need, you don't say, "I'm sorry, but I don't pray again until I go to bed tonight." Of course you wouldn't say that! In fact, we recommend that you pray with the person asking the request. That way you are sure to pray for their particulars rather than getting distracted with a busy schedule.

No longer is prayer a burden. It's a privilege to be able to pray not because of the law, but because of the grace of the cross.

Prayer: *Father God, what a privilege it is to pray without ceasing. You have given me the freedom to honor prayer at any time or any situation. May I be known as a person who prays. Amen.*

Action: Pray with a friend this week.

Today's Wisdom: *"Jesus' good news, then, was that the kingdom of God had come, and that he, Jesus, was its herald and expounder to men. More than that, in some special, mysterious way, he was the kingdom."*

    —Malcolm Muggeridge

God Is Bound By His Promises

*Keep watching and praying, that you
may not enter into temptation;
the spirit is willing, but the flesh is weak.*

—MATTHEW 26:41

od always keeps His promises. His character will not let Him fall back. In truth, all prayers offered through His Son, Jesus, are bound to be heard. God finds joy in keeping His promises.

We live in a day where all aspects of life are being undermined by dishonesty. Families have lost most of their retirement funds because they believed executives' promises that were made with their fingers crossed behind their backs.

Oh, how desperate is our country for people with character. We look to our sports heroes, our political leaders, our corporate leadership, the stars of movie and television, and even our spiritual leaders, hoping they will show us how people of character live. Each time we feel comfortable that a certain personality has the answer, we are disappointed by some worldly revelation of broken dreams and promises.

We expect people to do what they say they are going to do. We are disappointed when a plumber, an electrician, a painter, or a coworker can't do what they've said they are going to do. They miss the appointment or don't deliver their product on time—and here we patiently wait and nothing happens. Even parents tell their children that such-and-such will happen on Saturday, and it doesn't happen as promised. How many children go to their rooms to cry because a promise was broken?

We are so thankful that we have one who never goes back on His promises. God the Father, Jesus the Son, and the Holy Spirit always keep their word. If they said it, you can believe it. Let's all learn from the master of character to "just do what you say you are going to do."

Prayer: *Father God, thanks for being a promise keeper. You are the model for all of us. You give me great confidence in Your Word because I know You won't break a promise. If You said it, I believe it. Amen.*

Action: Make and keep a promise today—even a small one. Make this practice a discipline of your faith.

Today's Wisdom: *"Now to the King eternal, immortal, invisible, the only God, be honor and glory forever and ever. Amen."*

—1 Timothy 1:17

Thy Will Be Done,
on Earth As It Is in Heaven
A petition for God's kingdom to be among mankind

This third petition in the Lord's Prayer is a logical consequence after "hallowed be thy name" and "thy kingdom come." We know that in heaven the will of God is perfect—always has been and always will be. When God's earthly kingdom is established, He will do it through us believers. As earthlings, humans can't wait to glorify and magnify His holy name. We are anxiously waiting.

When this happens, the will of God will be done on earth as it is done in heaven. The Scriptures indicate that there will be a new heaven and a new earth.

C.S. Lewis wrote in *The Great Divorce*: "There are only two kinds of people in the end; those who say to God 'Thy will be done,' and those to whom God says in the end, 'thy will be done'—even if the end result is complete separation from God." Yet he also added, "No soul that seriously and constantly desires joy will ever miss it!" We are not robots. God has given each of us a will of our own; however, He does desire that our own individual will be in agreement with His divine and holy purpose.

When God's will and ours come together, we can have inward peace and share it with others. Then we are capable of truly loving our neighbors as unto ourselves.

One of Jesus' great promises is found in Romans 14:11, which says, "Every knee shall bow to Me, and every tongue shall give praise to God." Hallelujah! "Thy will be done."

> *God's purposes will ripen fast,*
> *Unfolding every hour;*
> *The bud may have a bitter taste,*
> *But sweet will be the flower.*
> *God is His own Interpreter,*
> *And He will make it plain.*

—William Cowper

You Have Joy

I have told you all this so that you will have
peace of heart and mind. Here on earth you will have
many trials and sorrows; but cheer up,
for I have overcome the world.

—JOHN 16:33 TLB

We want to share this with you so that you will
have peace of heart and mind. Joy *always* fol-
lows sorrow. We've met so many people who
are right in the middle of sorrow—a death, a separation, a
divorce, a serious health problem, teenage children that are
rebelling, financial difficulties, an unbelieving mate. The list
goes on and on.

Each of us, at one time or the other, has been in deep
sorrow. Sometimes it seems as if we will never smile again
because the burden is so heavy and the load is so great. In
our deepest sorrow, we have pleaded to God, "Restore to me
the joy of Thy salvation" (Psalm 51:12). The load then
becomes lighter, and we can pray to God to continue our joy
even during our deepest times of trouble.

Prayer: *Father God, joy is a decision on my part, and I'm*
committed to not letting anyone take it away from
me. Amen.

Action: Do something today that will spread your joy to someone who needs it.

Today's Wisdom:

Isn't life glorious! Isn't it grand!
Here—take it—hold it tightly in your hand;
Squeeze every drop of it into your soul,
Drink of the joy of it, sun-sweet and whole!
Laugh with the love of it, burst into song!
Scatter its richness as you stride along!
Isn't life splendid—and isn't it great
We can always start living—it's never too late!

—Helen Lowrie Marshall

□ □ □

Pray Expectantly

*Be anxious for nothing, but in everything by prayer
and supplication with thanksgiving let your requests
be made known to God.*

—Philippians 4:6

Prayer is not an imagination of the mind. It is real. Do we expect God to answer our prayers? I mean *really* expect Him to? We should anticipate answered prayer the moment we make our requests. It is God who gives us our desires, and He is already planning on answering them before the petitions leave our mouths. Thank God for His mercies and grace as soon as you pray.

When we have asked for our daily bread, take no more care, but believe that God has heard you and will give it to you. When you have taken your sick child before God, believe that the child will recover—or if not, that it will be a greater blessing to you and more glory to God. Leave it to Him.

In the early phase of Emilie's sickness, we claimed the Scripture verse John 11:4 which states, "This sickness is not unto death, but for the glory of God, that the Son of God may be glorified by it," with the full knowledge that if Emilie lived, the Son of God would be glorified, or if she did not live He would still be glorified. It's been amazing the reaction people have when they know that Emilie is being healed from cancer. All conversation changes to that topic. So many people and families are affected by this dreaded disease, and everyone wants to know how, when, and where. It's a common topic to be discussed. During our conversations we have great opportunities to give glory to God for the miracles and peace in our lives. We also praise our doctors, hospitals, medicine, nurses, lab technicians, and everyone else who is a part of Emilie's healing.

Even in sickness we are able to praise God for all He does for us.

Prayer: *Father God, You begin to answer my prayers even before they are uttered. I know from experience that You really care for me. May Your Son continue to be praised from my lips. Amen.*

Action: What affliction have you not yet turned into a chance to glorify God? Look for God's hand in the situation, and the peace will soon follow.

Today's Wisdom: *"If our petitions are in accordance with His will, and if we seek His glory in the asking, the answers will come in ways that will astonish us and fill our hearts with songs of thanksgiving."*

—J.K. Maclean

More Than We Ask For

*Now to Him who is able to do exceeding abundantly
beyond all that we ask or think, according
to the power that works within us,
to Him be the glory....*

—EPHESIANS 3:20-21

We are inspired by Scripture when it tells us that God will carry us through the valley of the shadow of death, through the fiery furnace, through plagues, through disasters, and through the battles. With all that harms us, He provides an escape. There are several verses that give us the assurance that He is a God of deliverance:

- You came near when I called you, and you said, "Do not fear." O LORD, you took up my case; you redeemed my life (Lamentations 3:57-58 NIV).

- I called upon the LORD in distress: The LORD answered me, and set me in a broad place (Psalm 118:5 NKJV).

- Then they cried unto the LORD in their trouble, and he delivered them out of their distresses. And he led them forth by the right way, that they might go to a city of habitation (Psalm 107:6-7 KJV).

We must discipline ourselves to study and know God's Word. Exciting results will come later when our hearts begin to produce a harvest of goodness and tranquility. After a while, we become strong and are able to help others.

In my recent journey of despair, I (Emilie) had reached the end of the road (so I thought). There was one ray of hope available—a bone-marrow transplant. We tried to match with my brother, our son, and our daughter; none worked. We sent out an S.O.S. for a donor and back came a perfect match from a 23-year-old Canadian male. He didn't know me, and I didn't know him, but God knew us both. I was accepted by the Fred Hutchinson Cancer Research Center in Seattle, Washington, to be a nonrelated bone-marrow recipient for a new protocol for patients over 55 years old. I was blessed by God to successfully receive healthy bone marrow from this young man.

God truly gave us more than we could have ever expected.

Prayer: *Father God, truly You give beyond my expectations. I praise You for my answered prayers. Amen.*

Action: Allow God to dream big on your behalf. Expect more from your Christian life.

Today's Wisdom: *"For God so loved the world, that He gave His only begotten Son, that whoever believes in Him should not perish, but have eternal life."*

—John 3:16

Just Ask

"What do you want Me to do for you?"

—MARK 10:51

hen our two children hesitated to ask me for something, I would tell them, "The worst I can say is no." Our son, Brad, didn't seem to take advantage of this guideline, but Jenny, our daughter, soon learned to ask for everything. The odds were in her favor that I would say yes more often than no.

God says He wants to give us the desires of our hearts. Many times we fall victim to negative thinking that prevents us from asking because we think God won't bless us with our requests. But God is *waiting* to hear our petitions and supplications. We shouldn't hold back because our faith is so small. We can humbly go to God—seeking His will for our lives. God will not give us something that would be harmful to us. And we wouldn't want anything that would not be beneficial to our Christian growth, right?

Throughout Scripture there are illustrations that tell us we are to ask:

> ❧ King Ahasuerus asked. "Queen Esther, What is your petition? It will be given you. What is your request?" (Esther 7:2 NIV).

> ❧ Solomon prayed for an understanding heart to discern between good and evil, and "the Lord

was pleased that Solomon had asked for this" (1 Kings 3:9-10 NIV).

❧ Jesus asked the blind man, "What do you want Me to do for you?" (Mark 10:51).

God is waiting for us to express our desires. Often we don't have something because we don't ask. Instead of approaching God with a small coffee mug, let's expand our faith and boldly go to Him with a big iced tea pitcher. Fill us up, Lord.[2]

Prayer: *Father God, help me have faith in Your promises that You want to hear our prayers. Let me not ask for things that would not be good for me. I want Your will to be done in my life. Amen.*

Action: Express yourself to the Lord. Share with Him your desires, and pray for His will and His leading.

Today's Wisdom: *"If my people who are called by my name humble themselves and pray, and seek my face and turn from their wicked ways, then I will hear from heaven, will forgive their sins, and will heal their land."*

—2 Chronicles 7:14

Be a Spiritual Worshiper

*Give ear to my prayer, O God; And do not hide
Thyself from my supplication.*

—PSALM 55:1

s I (Emilie) approach God in either public or private prayer, I must remember that this is an appointed time between me and my Lord. I must not flower my speech with babbling words that are meaningless or ones that puff me up before those who hear me talk with God.

As Jesus shared with His disciples the proper approach to prayer by giving them the Lord's Prayer (Matthew 6:9-13), we in turn are exhibiting how to pray for those watching around us. Be humble as you approach and worship the Lord.

During these last few years I have had the privilege of having many, many people pray for me. I have always been so blessed when those who came to visit asked, "Would you mind if I prayed for you?" "Of course not," came my immediate reply. Often the most powerful prayers were those uttered by God-fearing, humble warriors of the faith. Many of these were people who have traveled down the same road I traveled. They understood the suffering I experienced. They know the comforts of words that soothe the hurts of any illness. From years of their own suffering that has taken them to the foot of the cross, they are able to go directly to

God. He hears and responds with a blessing. Each petition has an impact upon our heavenly Father. He listens with an open ear to those who are lowly in spirit.

Prayer:
Father God, I am so very fortunate to have faithful prayer warriors come to You on my behalf. Such dear supporters. Thank You for acting upon their requests. May I also be as faithful. Amen.

Action:
Ask someone to pray for you today. Reflect on who needs prayer in your life. Commit to being a prayer warrior for him or her.

Today's Wisdom:
"I have resolved to pray more and pray always, to pray in all places where quietness inviteth, in the house, on the highway, and on the street; and to know no street or passage in this city that may not witness that I have not forgotten God."

—Sir Thomas Browne

The Perfect Manual

*But where can wisdom be found? And where is
the place of understanding?*

—JOB 28:12

ot long ago my friend Florence Littauer wrote a book titled *Looking for Love in All the Wrong Places*. And it's true. We look for love in all the wrong places—we seek wisdom in places where there is no wisdom by talking to friends, reading magazines, listening to talk shows, and attending seminars. We live in a culture that has a difficult time reading the instruction manual. For some reason we want to invent the wheel by ourselves. We have trouble seeking the truth from the wise.

The writer of the book of Job struggled with knowing what to do. In Job 28:12 he asked, "Where can wisdom be found?" All through chapter 28 he searched for the answer:

⇛ Man doesn't know its value (13).

⇛ It is not found in the land of the living (13).

⇛ The inner earth says, "It's not in me" (14).

⇛ The sea says, "It's not in me" (14).

⇛ You can't buy it with gold or silver (15).

⇛ Precious stones don't have it (16).

⇛ It can't be equated with gold (17).

- ❧ Pearls don't have it (18).

- ❧ It is hidden from the eyes of all living creatures (21).

- ❧ God understands its way, and He knows its place (23).

- ❧ God looks to the ends of the earth and sees everything under heaven (24).

- ❧ God saw wisdom and declared it (27).

- ❧ God established it and searched it out (27).

Job and his friends claimed wisdom of themselves, but wisdom is clearly an outgrowth of God and not merely something to be obtained. Although we can know and understand many things, we cannot attain the level of Creator wisdom. There will always be questions that only God can answer. Solomon knew that true wisdom is not found in human understanding but is from God alone (see Proverbs 1:7; 9:10).[3]

Prayer: *Father God, protect me from looking in all the wrong places for Your wisdom. Let me go to Your Word for all the answers to life's questions. Amen.*

Action: Go to the source of true wisdom—commit to reading the Bible daily for at least one month.

Today's Wisdom: *"Behold, the fear of the Lord, that is wisdom."*

    —Job 28:28

May Your Prayers Have Enlarged Expectations

*For My thoughts are not your thoughts, neither are
your ways My ways," declares the LORD.*

—ISAIAH 55:8

ince we have a great God on a great throne, we can take our petitions to Him. Often we are shy with our requests because we don't want to inconvenience God—so we give Him little requests. Paul prays in Ephesians 3:20, "Now to Him who is able to do exceeding abundantly beyond all that we ask or think, according to the power that works within us." Note the three biggies here:

- ❧ exceeding

- ❧ abundantly

- ❧ beyond all that we ask or think

Ephesians 3:20 challenges us to enlarge our expectations beyond our wildest dreams. But please note that there is one condition:

- ❧ according to the power that works within us

This power is the Holy Spirit. We're back to the principle, "Thy will be done."

Oh, God, give me proper faith that I can pray bigger prayers than I could ever think. At times I've put You into such a small box. It's hard for me to expand my thoughts upward to Your level of thought for me. When I (Emilie) was first diagnosed with lymphoma, a dear soul shared with me, "This sickness is not unto death, but for the glory of God, that the Son of God may be glorified by it" (John 11:4). See, I'd already died to the "Big C," but this verse gave me an encouragement to think beyond cancer and death. It gave me hope that I would live and my life would bring glory to God.

I no longer was eating the crumbs that fell on the floor. I was capable of walking the palace floor in the presence of God. My faith was expanded so I had enlarged expectations for my prayer requests. I expanded my vision of God to a greater dimension.

Prayer: *Father God, You are able to do exceeding abundantly, beyond all that I ask or think. Thank You for challenging me to bring enlarged expectations to You. May I glorify You in all that I do. Amen.*

Action: Think big today. Let God out of that limited box, and expand your view of His power and might.

Today's Wisdom: *"Do not be anxious for your life, as to what you shall eat, or what you shall drink; nor for your body, as to what you shall put on. Is not life more than food, and the body more than clothing?"*

—Matthew 6:25

Finding Favor in God's Eyes

Noah found favor in the eyes of the LORD. . . .
Thus Noah did; according to all that
God had commanded him.

—GENESIS 6:8,22

*I*f you were to pick up today's paper, you'd probably find a story about someone being honored for something he or she did. The accomplishment of someone in government, sports, medicine, education, theater, or music is being acknowledged by peers or even the world in general. Man finding favor with man is not unusual.

Have you ever thought about how much richer life would be to have God find favor with you? It's awesome to think of our holy God finding favor in us! Today's reading gives us an example of this.

Noah lived in a sin-filled world much like ours today. (We human beings haven't changed much over the centuries, we just call sin something else.) Despite the wickedness around him, Noah lived a life that was pleasing to God. It's important to realize that Noah didn't find favor because of his individual goodness, but because of his faith in God. You and I are judged by that same standard—are we faithful and obedient to God?

Although Noah was upright and blameless before God, he wasn't perfect. Genuine faith is not always perfect faith.

But despite his human failings, "Noah walked with God" (verse 9). The circumstances of Noah's life could have blocked that fellowship, but his heart qualified him to find favor with God.

Are you seeking favor with God or the favor and honor of man? Noah wanted only to please God. Know that when you go to God and admit that you are a sinner, you are pleasing God. At that time, you find His grace and move into a closer relationship with Jesus Christ. May you take steps like this to find favor in God's sight just as Noah did.

Prayer: *Father God, what an honor for Noah to have found favor in Your eyes! Help me to be faithful and obedient to You so that You might find favor with me. Give me a renewed hunger for Your Word so that I will know what You want from me. Help me be faithful to Your commands. Amen.*[4]

Action: Find a way to show your faithfulness to the Lord today. Seek His favor.

Today's Wisdom: *"Let your light shine before men in such a way that they may see your good works, and glorify your Father who is in heaven."*

—Matthew 5:16

Slow Down

I will lie down and sleep in peace, for you alone,
O LORD, make me dwell in safety.

—PSALM 4:8 NIV

We don't want to get into the trap of doing something just because it's the thing to do. We want to live a life that is meaningful to us and our family. We want our decisions to be based on our Christian values. We want to make decisions according to these values, not according to what the TV, Madison Avenue, or news reports tell us to do.

In order to live intuitively, we must have some quiet time to read and think. Hectic lives don't permit us to hear the heartbeat of the soul. When we are too busy, we don't have time to dwell on the important issues in life. When we're rushed, we have an inner disturbance that prevents us from making well-thought-out decisions. When you and I are hurried in life, we have a tendency to have deep anger because we forget to have time for ourselves. Our personal growth comes to a standstill. When this happens, *slow down.*

Prayer: Father God, let me be in tune with the feelings of my heart. Let me appreciate this time to know who I am and what I feel. Amen.

Action: Give yourself ten minutes today to express your feelings to God.

Today's
Wisdom: The Difference

I got up early one morning
and rushed into the day;
I had so much to accomplish
that I didn't have time to pray.

Problems just tumbled about me,
and heavier came each task.
"Why doesn't God help me?" I wondered.
He answered, "You didn't ask."

I wanted to see joy and beauty,
but the day toiled on, gray and bleak;
I wondered why God didn't show me.
He said, "But you didn't seek."

I tried to come into God's presence,
I used all my keys at the lock.
God gently and lovingly chided,
"My child, you didn't knock."

I woke up early this morning,
and paused before entering the day;
I had so much to accomplish
that I had to take time to pray.

—Grace L. Naessens

Give Us This Day Our Daily Bread

A petition for our needs and desires

In this fourth petition of our Lord's Prayer, we are introduced to the idea that God is interested in our daily needs—that of providing food for our bodies.

Right after Jesus puts emphasis on the three petitions dealing with *God:* hallowed be *Thy* name, *Thy* kingdom come, and *Thy* will be done, we see that Jesus is concerned about our bodily needs for survival—our daily bread. He knows that if our bodily needs are not met there will be no need to fulfill our mental and spiritual needs. Man is alive, and he must be kept alive.

The word "bread" is not limited to the literal meaning, but can be expanded to all the necessities of life. It covers all of our material needs—everything that is necessary for us to live. What is meant by daily bread? All that belongs to the wants and support of the body, such as meat, drink, clothing, shoes, house, home, land, cattle, money, pious spouse, pious children, pious and faithful leaders, good government, good weather, peace, health, order, honor, good friends, trusty neighbors, and the like. Also consider that our prayer is not for two, three, or four days of provision, but just for one—today.

Just think, God is concerned about the very smallest of our everyday needs. Scripture says that He is concerned about the hairs on our heads. This awesome God concerns Himself about the littlest of our needs. He is even aware when a small sparrow falls to the ground, and we are certainly more important to God than the birds in the air.

Much emphasis must be made that we are to pray for our basic necessities and not for all of our wants. God promises to provide the basic necessities but He makes no promises for luxuries. One of the basics of life is that if we are faithful in little things, God will give us dominion over many things.

Even though God provides our daily necessities, we must acknowledge that all these provisions come from Him. Each day take time to pause and thank God for all He has given us. We must always realize our utter dependence upon the almighty God. We would have nothing if it were not for His grace. He wills for all good blessings to occur.

> *Be present at our table, Lord;*
> *Be here and everywhere adored.*
> *The children bless, and grant that we*
> *May feast in fellowship with Thee.*

> —Isaac Watts

The Comforter

*What a wonderful God we have—he is the Father
of our Lord Jesus Christ, the source of every mercy,
and the one who so wonderfully comforts
and strengthens us in our hardships and trials.*

—2 CORINTHIANS 1:3-4 TLB

ometimes we stroll along life's busy highways with good health, humming a song, without a trouble in the world. All systems are go. Suddenly a trial raises its ugly head, and we come to a screeching halt. Red lights flash everywhere. *Help!* What do we do?

We know what we did! We began to pray. Lord, for whatever we receive now and what we will receive in the future—pain as well as joy—please teach us the secret of giving thanks. For what we have already received—what has shaped our lives in the past, and what is shaping us today—please fill our lives with thanksgiving. May we reach out and encourage other lives that are in similar circumstances with the same comfort that You have bestowed upon us.

When we step down off the throne and invite Jesus there, we are more open to see what the Holy Spirit is trying to teach us through our circumstances.

Prayer: Father God, I need courage. You have great things
for me to do; You have put dreams in my heart.
Show me, Lord, what to do next. I only want to
follow You. Amen.

Action: Pray about your situation. Feel the presence
of the Comforter.

*Today's
Wisdom:*
I thank God and I praise Him
for the sunset that lifts my spirit,
the morning that lets my
soul take flight in search
of wildflowers, the songbirds that
waken my world. And I
thank God for His presence
in my life, for family and friends,
for joy and even for sorrows
that strengthen my life, for
the awareness that
God's love is the essence of
all happiness, the bond between
heaven and earth.

—Neil C. Fitzgerald

David's Prayer of Repentance

*Restore to me the joy of your salvation and grant
me a willing spirit, to sustain me.*

—PSALM 51:12 NIV

In Psalm 51, David pleads for forgiveness and cleansing (verses 1-2), confesses his guilt (verses 3-6), prays for pardon and restoration (verses 7-12), resolves to praise God (verses 13-17), and prays for the continued prosperity of Jerusalem (verses 18-19). This psalm elaborates David's confession of his sin with Bathsheba (see 2 Samuel 11–12, with emphasis on 12:3).

Psalm 51 highlights the highs of victory and the lows of defeat. As sinners, we can appreciate how heavy David's heart was and his desire to approach his heavenly Father to ask forgiveness. We can relate to his longing to be restored in his daily walk of uprightness in the presence of God.

Read all of Psalm 51 in the NIV translation. This is a confession to meditate over. Chew it up and digest it. Certain words and phrases will surely touch your soul:

- Have mercy on me.
- Blot out my transgressions (sins).
- I have sinned against You.
- Cleanse me and make me whiter than snow.
- Let me again hear joy and gladness.

◦ Blot out my iniquity.

◦ Create in me a pure heart.

◦ Renew a steadfast spirit within me.

◦ Restore my joy of Your salvation.

◦ Give me a willing spirit.

◦ My tongue will sing of Your righteousness.

◦ Open my lips and mouth for praise.

◦ Give me a broken and contrite heart.

As you examine this confession, you see a man who has been broken and begs for restoration. We have never been to the depths of David's despair, but our sins have brought us to the place where we cry out to God, "Please forgive me, a helpless sinner."⁵

Prayer: *Father God, I want to give You all of my known and unknown sins today. I don't want to leave Your presence with any unconfessed sin in my life. I want to go away with a clean heart and with Your joy of forgiveness in me. Only by Your grace have You protected me from the ugliness of sin. Please be with those who read today's psalm, so that they too will know of Your grace, love, and forgiveness. Amen.*

Action: Confess your sins, and seek a right spirit before the Lord.

Today's Wisdom: *"Taking the five loaves and the two fish and looking up to heaven, he gave thanks and broke the loaves. Then he gave them to his disciples to set before the people."*

—Mark 6:41 NIV

Enter Prayer with Lowly Reverence

I came that they might have life,
and might have it abundantly.

—JOHN 10:10

If in prayer we come to God's throne, it is obvious that our attitude should be one of humble reverence. The whole universe respects the power of God's radiance. Before the creation of the world He was. Just think before mountains, oceans, deserts, rain, floods, earthquakes—He was. We're not sure we can understand how powerful God is—our earthly minds can't comprehend His thoughts.

We can easily see that we shouldn't flippantly approach God in a casual fashion. We must prepare our souls as we enter into prayer. I (Emilie) have never been so humble as I am now. For once in my life, I've begun to experience God as He intended me to. With many doctor and hospital visits under my belt, all vanity has been stripped away. Have you also experienced a situation that required humility and vulnerability?

Through these experiences we can begin to understand how God wants us to approach His throne. Through difficult, soul-exposing circumstances, God teaches us to pray effectively. I know that the content of my prayers are a lot different than before my illness. God's name is hallowed, and He is truly my majestic King.

Prayer: Father God, I want to be reverent toward You when I come into Your presence. In a society where we are dumbing down, I want to raise You up to Your status of King. Amen.

Action: Be vulnerable to God about something you have been silent about. Approach His throne with the humility you have learned through life's difficult times.

Today's Wisdom: "Instruct those who are rich in this present world not to be conceited or to fix their hope on the uncertainty of riches, but on God, who richly supplies us with all things to enjoy."

—1 Timothy 6:17

The Minimum Daily Adult Requirement

For it is by grace you have been saved, through
faith—and this not from yourselves, it is the gift of
God—not by works, so that no one can boast.

—EPHESIANS 2:8-9 NIV

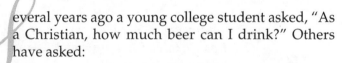everal years ago a young college student asked, "As a Christian, how much beer can I drink?" Others have asked:

- How long should I read my Bible each day?

- How long should I pray each day?

- How much money do I have to give to the church?

- How many times a week must I be in church?

- Do I have to _____ , _____ , _____?

We're interested in daily nutritional requirements when it comes to our food, so it makes sense that we are concerned when it comes to our Christian walk and our spiritual health. What is the minimum daily adult requirement for being a Christian? What do we really have to do to get by? We want to know exactly what we need to do in order to be a true Christian.

Paul addresses these very basic concerns in his letter to the Ephesians. He very clearly states one of the main principles in today's verse. Paraphrased, he said, "Christ has freed us from bondage to minimum daily adult requirements. Our relationship with the Lord Jesus is not contingent on works; it is a gift of grace."

"So," you ask, "do I do nothing as a Christian? Aren't there any requirements?" Scripture challenges us to be like Christ, and if we are to do that, we need to open the Bible and learn how Jesus lived. When we do so, we see that Jesus studied God's Word, spent time with believers, prayed regularly, and served those around Him. He did all these things not out of obligation but out of love.

So what is your minimum daily adult requirement when it comes to spiritual health?[6]

Prayer: *Father God, help me not to worry about "how long" or "how often" as I try to live a life that pleases You. Put a strong desire in my soul to spend time with You today in prayer and study not so that I am doing what I "should," but because I love. Amen.*

Action: Let your loving God guide you through your day, and let Him shape your spiritual life.

Today's Wisdom: *The blessing of God rests upon all those who have been kind to us, have cared for us, have worked for us, have served us, and have shared our bread at this table. Our merciful God, reward all of them in Your own way, for Yours is the glory and the honor forever.*

—St. Cyril of Alexandria

Receive All of God's Blessings

*And if ye walk contrary unto me . . . will
I also walk contrary unto you.*

—LEVITICUS 26:21,24 KJV

"And whatsoever we ask, we receive of Him, because we keep His commandments" (1 John 3:22 KJV). Any responsible father can tell you that you cannot grant to a disobedient child his wishes. If the father does, then he can't manage his family properly. Sadly there comes a time when the parent must insist that if the child is not obedient to rules of the home or does not listen to the wisdom of the parent, then the child will have to go somewhere else.

God acts toward us as we act to our wayward child. It's not that He doesn't love us, but He responds with "tough love" because He loves us so much. The child is still a member of the family, but he will not receive the many blessings afforded him because he was disobedient to wisdom and truth.

We are amazed when we meet individuals who don't look or act like Christians, but in conversation they share that they attended church when they were younger and accepted Jesus as their personal Savior. Their present lives certainly don't reflect those early childhood decisions, yet they still classify themselves as Christians.

God is longing for them to return to His way. He wants them—and each of us—to share in His great blessings—all of them!

Prayer: *Father God, if I'm going to be identified with You, then I should be obedient to who You are. I don't want to stand before You at judgment day and hear you say, "Depart from Me. I never knew you." Amen.*

Action: Stand up for God today. Stand as God's light in the world's darkness.

Today's Wisdom: *"Yet ye have forsaken me, and served other gods: wherefore I will deliver you no more. Go and cry unto the gods which ye have chosen."*

—Judges 10:13-14 KJV

Praise God Joyously

Oh, send out your light and your truth—
let them lead me. Let them lead me to your Temple
on your holy mountain, Zion. There I will go
to the altar of God, my exceeding joy,
and praise him with my harp. O God—my God!

—PSALM 43:3-4 TLB

et Jesus' light and your present situation lead you to truth that will put you in the presence of God. I (Emilie) have met countless people who have found Jesus through their journey of pain or loss. I have also witnessed a few who have rejected the truth. Most of this latter group cut themselves off from their support groups and live in isolation and loneliness.

Even though I came into my personal difficult journey with my Christian faith, I have experienced an abundance of growth in my Christian walk. I have found that my altar to God is in my prayer closet. I didn't spend time considering whether my coffee was weak or strong, or had too much or too little cream. The little things of life never appeared on the radar screen, I was able to sing praises to God's name. This grander view of what is important opens my eyes to the needs of others and God's goodness in the midst of these needs.

Prayer: *Father God, as I go through this journey called life, let me be open to Your light and truth. Let my spirit be open to all You want to teach me. Stretch me beyond where I've ever been before. Amen.*

Action: What difficult trial do you face? Look for God's light in this situation. It is there.

Today's Wisdom: "*Real, cleansing forgiveness is a forgetting—a real canceling out of the past. When a hurt is forgiven, it is as if it never happened; it is gone—forgotten as a dream—never to return.*"

—A. Philip Parcham

Stop Worrying

*Will all your worries
add a single moment to your life?*

—Matthew 6:27 TLB

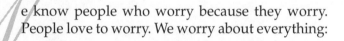

e know people who worry because they worry. People love to worry. We worry about everything:

- Will I have enough money to pay the bills?
- Will the children stay out of trouble?
- Does my spouse love me?
- Is my job secure?

Eighty-five percent of the things we worry about never happen. We tire ourselves out by using our positive energy on negative issues. Stop worrying and start resolving your concerns with positive endeavors. Concentrate on issues you can do something about.

- Pray more
- Praise more
- Love more
- Laugh more
- Take a cooking class

🕊 Go to a good play

🕊 Be a friend

Stop thinking negatively; sing a new song. Let God know that you are trusting Him to give you clear direction in your life. Don't get caught up in an ulcer-producing, peace-destroying lifestyle. Worry is not God's best for us. Worry doesn't keep bad things from happening—it just prevents us from enjoying the good things in life.

Prayer: *Father God, I want to stop worrying. Let me be brave in this decision. Let me move forward with the assurance that You will handle my every need. Amen.*

Action: Write down one worry you have today. Now cross it out and write above it one positive thing you will do instead of focusing on that concern.

Today's Wisdom: *"For the sake of your Son Jesus Christ, have mercy on us and forgive us; that we may delight in your will, and walk in your ways, to the glory of your name. Amen."*

—The Book of Common Prayer

Words That Encourage

For everything that was written in the past
was written to teach us, so that through endurance
and the encouragement of the Scriptures
we might have hope.

—ROMANS 15:4 NIV

Never in my life have I (Emilie) enjoyed reading God's Word as much as in the past five years of trials. I'm not reading to take notes or to prepare for a seminar; I'm just taking in the sweet words, verse after verse, that have brought me such encouragement.

I especially appreciate those passages brought to my attention by loving friends who send cards and letters. Many of these day-brighteners include a reference to a passage that has had meaning to the sender. As I read and meditate on these precious words, my soul is refreshed with a new sense of God's promises and faithfulness. Even familiar passages take on new meaning, and I enjoy them like never before. I've even started writing names and dates in the margins of my Bible beside certain special passages. That way I will always have a record of when this reading was brought to my attention and who cared enough to share it with me.

Revisiting Scriptures that have had meaning at different points in my life serves to remind me of God's presence throughout the trials and joys of a lifetime. This security offers me assurance that God will be with me every step of the way. Believers are the recipients of such hope!

Prayer: *Father God, I so appreciate the verses that are brought to my attention. Let me dwell on Your holy words. May I taste the sweetness of Your comforting wisdom. Let me seek ways to invite Your Word into my life and the lives of those around me. Amen.*

Action: Choose a passage of Scripture to pray out loud. Read it and pray on it three times over the course of the day.

Today's Wisdom: *"Without the burden of afflictions, it is impossible to reach the height of grace. The gifts of grace increase as the struggles increase."*

—St. Rose of Lima

Choose Whom You Will Serve

*And if it is disagreeable in your sight to serve the
LORD, choose for yourselves today whom you will
serve: whether the gods which your fathers served
which were beyond the River, or the gods of the
Amorites in whose land you are living; but as for me
and my house, we will serve the LORD.*

—JOSHUA 24:15

Prayer is not a hard requirement—it is the natural
privilege of a person to his Creator. To those of us
who do pray, it is a precious time, for it is the way
that God sends down blessings to us and the way that He
answers our needs.

Anything that hinders us from prayer is wrong. Nothing
during our daily duties is more important than our time in
prayer. If at all possible we encourage husbands and wives
to pray together. As a family if we are not joined together in
prayer, how can we expect to receive all of God's blessings
for us?

We must seek God's guidance if we are to accomplish
our goals in life. If we don't model a prayer life in our homes,
our children will grow up indifferent to our faith and, in
many cases, they will reject our Christianity.

Life is made up of decisions and choices. Much of what
we are is a compilation of choices we have made over our
lifetimes. If we make bad choices we usually end up in a bad

way; however, we find that successful people have a history of making good choices.

In our Scripture verse today we see that Joshua had a big decision to make. Which god was he to choose? This is basically the same decision for us. Which god will we choose? The choice you make will determine your eternal destiny.

Parents will be eternally judged by how well they teach their children in the faith. Paul, in Romans 12:2, commands us not to be "conformed to this world, but be transformed by the renewing of your minds, that you may prove what the will of God is."

Prayer: *Father God, you chose me, now I choose You. I truly want to serve You as my Lord and Savior. Help me lead my family in Your ways. Amen.*

Action: Be deliberate in your faith today. Share with your child or family a time of prayer.

Today's Wisdom: *"Our Father, who art in heaven, bless the provisions of Thy bounty now set before us, and feed our souls with the bread of life, for Christ's sake. Thou hast again supplied our returning wants. Continue, we pray Thee, to be our God and keeper, supply the wants of the destitute, and fill the earth with Thy glory, for Christ's sake. Amen."*

           —from Luther's Small Catechism

Mercy Bestowed in Gold

*My grace is sufficient for you, for power is
perfected in weakness.*

—2 CORINTHIANS 12:9

We must remember that our prayers are to be offered in submission to God's will for our lives. Just because God hears our prayers, doesn't mean He always gives us everything we ask for. However, He does give us everything that is good for us. All of our prayers should include, "Nevertheless, not as I will, but as thou wilt" (Matthew 26:39). Our will should always be God's will for us.

Martin Luther once said, "To have prayed well is to have studied well." This is a challenge we face—not to pray from a void of study. We are to study God's Word and understand Him. Knowing God's will for our lives is impossible unless we get to know the character of God. We know Him by being with Him in study and prayer. Only then can our prayers be like gold. Gold is purified by extreme heat that burns out all the impurities of the ore. Sometimes when we pray, God is saying in reply, "Not yet." God's timing is always perfect— never too soon and never too late. Trust Him!

Prayer: *Father God, I stand in awe as I approach Your
throne of grace this morning. There is so much I*

*don't know about You and all the spiritual dimen-
sions of life. I know You as my Savior. I want to
touch the nail prints in Your hands. I truly want
to touch You. Your sweat, Your compassion, Your
faith, Your trustworthiness. As I spend time with
You today, may my window of knowledge about
You swing wide open.*

*As I utter my feeble words upward, may I
screen them so there is no selfishness uttered on
my behalf. I so want my will to be Your will for my
life. May my prayers of silver be received as
requests of gold. Screen from my thoughts and
lips those words that would not be beneficial for
me.*

*Thank You, Lord, for giving an ear to my peti-
tions. You truly are a God worthy of praise.*

In Jesus' name I pray. Amen.

Action: Study God's Word today and focus on His
character.

*Today's
Wisdom:*   *"Be present at our table, Lord
Be here and everywhere adored.
These mercies bless, and grant that we
May feast in paradise with Thee."*

—John Cennick

And Forgive Our Debts, As We Also Have Forgiven Our Debtors

A petition for forgiveness to self and to others

In this fifth petition of our Lord's Prayer, we as believers are directed to pray for forgiveness of those everyday sins that we commit after salvation. Since we opened the Lord's Prayer with "Our Father," we are believers and are called His children. Immediately we are to approach the throne of God and confess our daily sins, at which time the Father will forgive and forget. If we know that we have been forgiven then we can forgive those who sin against us.

If we have accepted Jesus as our Savior, our hearts are tender and pliable and cannot be hard and brittle. We cannot and must not refuse forgiveness. "Jesus, as You can forgive me, I am able to forgive others. I can forgive because of what the cross has done for me."

In life we might be asked to forgive on some very big issues—ones that we don't know if we can. But when we think back at what Jesus did on the cross for us, we cannot refuse to forgive. God will give us the strength and courage to forgive.

Notice that the only point the Lord emphasizes in the prayer is the necessity for forgiving one another. Forgiveness with the Father depends on forgiveness among the members of the family of God. This is the forgiveness that affects fellowship within the family of God—not the forgiveness that leads to salvation.

Yet, forgiveness is not ignoring sin. We are to remain discerning people. Forgiveness is not simply looking the other way when we have been trespassed against. There are times when we must fully face the wrong done against us, confront the issue, and cast away the denial that nothing happened. When we face the reality of the wrong, then we can confess, cry, pray, and move on—forgetting the past.

Tough Times Don't Last

I said, "Sometimes I fail."
He said, "I'll see you through."
I said, "But what if I fall?"
He said, "I will carry you."

I said, "My fears are great!"
He said, "Trust Me alone."
I said, "But I'm depressed."
He said, "I'll cheer you on."

I said, "Life isn't easy."
He said, "Please let Me help.
Remember, I love you."
I said, "Lord, I accept."

—Perry Tanksley

From Worry to Prayer

Who among you fears the Lord?. . . Let them trust the Lord, let them rely upon their God.

—ISAIAH 50:10 TLB

Chuck Swindoll says there are six words that should clearly be fixed in our minds. These six words form the foundation of God's therapeutic process for all worry-warts.

> Worry About Nothing.
> Pray About Everything.

Worry is one of the great negatives for the mind. Americans waste so much time worrying! It literally drains all of the joy from our presence.

We have found that we need to take items from our "worry list" and put them on our "prayer list." Now *that's* a list we can do something about. Ruth Graham told a group of ladies, "Tell your husband the positive, and tell God the negative." Transfer your anxieties from worry to prayer. That way you can be proactive about your situation.

This is not just to say, "Let go and let God," but it is great to see how God handles the situation according to *His* will. We no longer have to manipulate the events of our lives. We can rest in His perfect will.

Prayer: *Father God, let me not forget those six great words. So simple, but so hard to do. I want to move from worry to prayer. Amen.*

Action: Start your day today with prayer. Give your immediate worries over to God. Let Him hold them for you today and enjoy the release of that burden.

Today's Wisdom: *God grant me the serenity to accept the things I cannot change; courage to change the things I can; and wisdom to know the difference.*

—The Serenity Prayer

Pray for a Friend

*It is only the Lord's mercies that have kept us
from complete destruction. Great is his faithfulness;
his loving-kindness begins afresh each day.*

—LAMENTATIONS 3:22-23 TLB

During the course of your day, pray for a friend. While you're resting, running errands, having your quiet time, or listening to music, take a moment to pray. Pray for wisdom for your friends who have children—they might need special insights as they raise those precious ones.

In Colossians 1:9-12, we find a wonderful model for friendship prayer. This prayer covers—

- having special wisdom and understanding

- walking in a manner worthy of the Lord

- bearing fruit in all good works

- increasing in the knowledge of God

- being strengthened with all power, for the attaining of all steadfastness and patience

Read the Colossians passage:

> For this reason also, since the day we heard of it,
> we have not ceased to pray for you and to ask
> that you may be filled with the knowledge of His

> will in all spiritual wisdom and understanding, so that you may walk in a manner worthy of the Lord, to please Him in all respects, bearing fruit in every good work and increasing in the knowledge of God; strengthened with all power, according to His glorious might, for the attaining of all steadfastness and patience; joyously giving thanks to the Father, who has qualified us to share in the inheritance of the saints in light (Colossians 1:9-12).

What an armor of protection and growth you can give your friend with a prayer like this! Let us tell you from experience—having friends praying for us brings tremendous comfort.

Prayer: *Father God, I give my friendships and my friends to You. They are wonderful gifts in my life. Please bless them today. Amen.*

Action: Write down in your journal a list of friends and family members you will pray for this month. Stay faithful to this prayer list.

Today's Wisdom: *"If therefore you are presenting your offering at the altar, and there remember that your brother has something against you, leave your offering there before the altar, and go your way; first be reconciled to your brother, and then come and present your offering."*

—Matthew 5:23-24

Let the Lord Bless You

May the Lord bless and protect you;
may the Lord's face radiate with joy because of you;
may he be gracious to you, show you his favor,
and give you his peace.

—NUMBERS 6:24-26 TLB

Knock the socks off all those you meet today when you give them this special blessing:

May the Lord bless you.
May the Lord keep you.
May the Lord shine upon you.
May the Lord be gracious to you.
May His countenance be given to you.

Whoever receives this blessing would consider themselves blessed. You know all of us could use such a daily blessing. We live in a world where finding peace and favor is becoming more difficult. Just look around, and you can find suffering everywhere.

The more you trust God, the more you will come to know His character and stare in amazement at what He's done in your life. You will anxiously wait in anticipation for what He's going to do next. And when God's character radiates from your face, hurting people will want to know your secret.

Prayer: *Father God, I know all blessings come from You. May I learn from You how to bless others. I want to reflect Your peace even when I feel restless and uptight. Relax me in Your presence. Amen.*

Action: Name three blessings from God that you have received this month. Tell others about these gifts.

Today's Wisdom: *"'Lord, how often shall my brother sin against me, and I forgive him? Up to seven times?' Jesus said to him 'I do not say to you up to seven times, but up to seventy times seven.'"*

—Matthew 18:21-22 NKJV

And They Went to Sleep

Cast your burden upon the LORD
and he will sustain you.

—PSALM 55:22

Have you heard about the man who owed his next door neighbor $100? The bill was due the next day, and the debtor only had $30. That night, the man was so anxious about the next morning that his tossing and turning kept his wife awake. Finally, exasperated, she got out of bed, threw open the window, and yelled to the neighbor, "Hey, Ruben! About the $100—he ain't got it!" "Now," she said to her husband, "let him worry!" And they both went to sleep.

Have you ever tossed and turned because you were worrying about a big burden? This worry keeps replaying itself in your head. You fret, lose your train of thought, and become stressed-out. If you will remember today's verse, you will relax and go to bed. When God says to cast your burden upon Him and He will sustain you, He means every word.

I (Emilie) have prayed more in the last five years than I've ever prayed. During this walk with cancer, God and I have become close friends. I've meekly prayed, and I've prayed with anger, tears, a pitched voice, petitions, praise, and thanksgiving. And God heard me each time and has sustained me.

He will sustain you, too. God delights in being our God. Don't rob Him of His joy. He delights to shoulder your burdens.

Prayer: *Father God, I want to be more transparent with my daily problems. You know what they are. Thanks for being concerned about every one. Amen.*

Action: Reveal to God what you need from Him.

Today's Wisdom: *Did you know you have an angel watching over you?*
Though you cannot see them, you can be sure it's true.
By day or by night, they guide you as you work and play;
Your Heavenly Father has provided for you in His loving way.

—Author unknown

Always the Dawn

*He lifts the burdens from those bent down beneath
their loads. For the Lord loves good men.*

—PSALM 146:8 TLB

o you ever think about what God's new morning message to us might be? Regardless of what the weather might be like—cloudy or sunny—the message is always the same. His promise is that the dawn will come at the beginning of each day. In all our troubles, He promises to be with us and to lift our burdens.

He wants to tell us that He will be alongside to help us through the day. He hasn't forgotten us. He knows our names. He understands our circumstances. He hears our every prayer. The dawn brings a new day that contains the same promises of yesterday. Even during the darkness of night, God is there. You can trust His presence. He never leaves or forsakes us. Each new day has its dawn.

Prayer: *Father God, I love the assurance that You are with me each day. In every situation, You keep Your promises. I'm so glad You help me with the day's load. Amen.*

Action: While driving or doing the dishes or waiting in the bank drive-thru line…talk to God. Stay aware of His presence throughout the day.

Today's Wisdom: *"Do not rejoice when your enemy falls, and do not let your heart be glad when he stumbles."*

—Proverbs 24:17

A Great Proclamation

The Lord is my strength, my song, and my salvation.
He is my God, and I will praise him.
He is my father's God—I will exalt him.

—EXODUS 15:2 TLB

Yuu don't need to feel defeated today. Instead, praise God and He will lift you up. You might not feel too excited about life this morning, but you are going to change all that. Today you must choose to be joyful! Remember, we're not going to let those negative thoughts get us down. We will rise above all that drags us into the pit of despair.

The Lord is our strength, our song, and our salvation. He has become our victory.

All through my journey, I've (Emilie) made a habit of spending time alone with God. Often I would have my Bob cozy up beside me on the bed to read me Scripture or to read from the pages of a devotional book. His strong presence was a great comfort to me. He has truly been my angelic caregiver. I don't know where I would be today without Bob's courage. When I would get down, he would come along and say the right words that would give me hope again. Our prayer times were and are very precious to us both. These trying times have brought us closer together and closer to God.

What draws you to the heart of God when you are in need? Do you pray alone? With others? God is right there beside you. Do not forget that His presence bathes you in a balm of hope when you are weary. There is no greater feeling than to be wrapped in the security of God's love.

Prayer: Father God, I so need you today. My spirit feels dry and lifeless. Nourish me, feed me with your Spirit, and comfort me through the truth of Your Word. Amen.

Action: Lift up a brother or sister in Christ with encouraging words today.

Today's Wisdom: "To love anyone is nothing else than to wish that person good."

—St. Thomas Aquinas

Call Me Anytime

The Lord has set apart the redeemed for himself.
Therefore he will listen to me
and answer when I call to him.

—PSALM 4:3 TLB

t is good to be able to call upon God anytime—morning, day, or night—and He will have time for us. We never get a busy signal when we call Him. He is more reliable than dialing 911. Just think...God has given us a direct line. What a privilege to be a child of God! Our Creator is always ready to listen to us.

There were many times we called out to God when we were at a fork in the road and weren't quite sure which path we should take. In each situation, He gave us clarity of thought. But the final decision was ours.

As with any promise, there is always a condition. In this Scripture, the promise is that God will always listen to and answer the redeemed. You meet this condition if you are one of His children.

As we get busy with details of taking care of our families, ourselves, and the day-to-day business of life, it is so easy to forget our direct line to our Savior. We are blessed to be cared for so deeply that our Maker desires our communication. He awaits our calls.

Prayer: Father God, thank You for hearing my every prayer. No matter how small it is to You, it's very big to me. I ask that all my prayers fit into Your will for my life. Amen.

Action: When you feel stressed today, think of God as your first contact.

Today's Wisdom: "We implore the mercy of God, not that He may leave us at peace in our vices, but that He may deliver us from them."

—Pascal

Friends Pray for Friends

*Dear friend, I am praying that all is well with you
and that your body is as healthy
as I know your soul is.*

—3 JOHN 1:2 TLB

Where would I (Emilie) be, if I didn't have praying friends? During my illness (almost five years now), I have had the privilege of receiving thousands of cards and letters from people in various walks of life. They have sent me the sweetest cards, telling me of their unending prayers for my health. These cards seem to come at the most opportune times. I needed that little encouragement that tells me I'm not fighting this fight alone.

One of my biggest thrills was when I received 1200 cards from the Bailey Smith Ministry in Atlanta, Georgia. I had been scheduled to speak at one of their seminars but because of my poor health, I had to cancel the engagement. However, they wrote me love letters, telling me how much I was missed and that they were petitioning God for a complete healing—this side of heaven.

Have you ever felt a tug at your heart specifically for someone? Or have you tossed and turned at night and found that beneath your restlessness were thoughts of a person in your life and his or her specific needs? Turn your worries or thoughts into prayers for those people. These times are truly gifts. Gifts for you and also for the recipient of your prayers.

Be an encouragement to those God has brought to your memory.

Prayer: *Father God, I understand so little of what You are trying to accomplish or how You work Your will. But I know You love me, and that's all I need to know. Amen.*

Action: In those moments when names come to mind, pause to lift the people up in prayer. Keep a record so that you can continue to pray for them over time.

Today's Wisdom: *"Nowhere can we get to know the holiness of God and come under its influence and power, except in the inner chambers. It has been well said: 'No man can expect to make progress in holiness who is not often and long alone with God.'"*

—Andrew Murray

You Are a Light

No one lights a lamp and hides it!
Instead, he puts it on a lampstand to
give light to all who enter the room.

—LUKE 11:33 TLB

n a small mountain village in Europe several centuries ago (so the story goes), a nobleman wondered what legacy to leave his townspeople. At last, he decided to build them a church.

Nobody saw the complete plans until the church was finished. When the people gathered, they marveled at its beauty. But one noticed it was incomplete.

"Where are the lamps?" he asked. "How will the church be lighted?"

The nobleman smiled. Then he gave each family a lamp. "Each time you are here, the area in which you sit will be illuminated. But when you are not here, some part of God's house will be dark."

Today we live in a world of darkness, navigating dim paths on which our secular problem-solvers stumble. The world is so big and our lamps are so small. True—but we can light some small part of every day. Each of us is a lamp. Together, we can make our world a brighter place. It all begins with the desire expressed in Michelangelo's prayer, "God, grant me the desire always to desire to be more than I can ever accomplish."

Prayer: *Father God, You are my lamp. May I always reflect Your love to the dark world as I pass through. I want to keep my lamp full of oil so my path will be lit by Your glow. Amen.*

Action: Today, focus on two things: being a light in your immediate setting and acknowledging the light of another.

Today's Wisdom: *"He went off to the mountain to pray, and He spent the whole night in prayer to God."*

—Luke 6:12

Don't Count Sheep

*I lie awake at night thinking of you—of how much
you have helped me—and how I rejoice through the
night beneath the protecting shadow of your wings.*

—PSALM 63:6-7 TLB

he world tells us to count sheep when we can't sleep.
But during the long nighttime hours when I (Emilie)
haven't been able to sleep, I've learned to pray and
meditate on the Scriptures.

I have found that not only is God the God of the daytime,
but He is also the God of nighttime. Some of my most precious hours come after the sun goes down. The stillness of
the evening gives me a wonderful opportunity to pray and
meditate on God's holy Word.

I have been amazed at the recall I have of people I
haven't thought of for a long time. When this occurs my
mind races back to all those fond memories I have of them.
Because I'm in no hurry and don't have any pressing
appointments, I can lavishly spend my time praying for
them and their families. Often I send them a card the next
day to let them know I prayed for them.

Perhaps there is someone in your life you need to forgive. Holding on to the grace of God, this is possible. We
have the perfect model of forgiveness and sacrifice as
believers. Extend this grace to another, and see how God

will change your heart toward that person and the circumstances.

Praying for your friends and family is a tremendous privilege. It does your heart good, and it encourages others to know you care enough to pray for them.

Prayer: *Father God, I'm tired of counting sheep. Now I can pray for those who need prayer. Help me focus my time to get to know You better. Amen.*

Action: Let go of the burden you carry today. Forgive someone through a simple prayer to the Lord. Experience this freedom and write about it in your journal.

Today's Wisdom: *"He who is too busy to pray will be too busy to live a holy life. Satan had rather we let the grass grow on the path to our prayer chamber than anything else."*

—E.M. Bounds

And Do Not Lead Us into Temptation, but Deliver Us from Evil

A petition that we would never be led into a situation where we are liable to be tempted by Satan

In this sixth petition of our Lord's Prayer, we are requesting from God that we should never be led into a circumstance or situation where we are likely to be tempted by Satan. The saints of Scripture have prayed for this protection throughout time. As human beings we will be comforted during trials that will test our character. Not that God puts us there, but that when we live life we will not be tempted. It is at this time we must pray, "Satan get behind me! Flee from me in the Name of Jesus!"

In 1 Corinthians 10:13 we read, "No temptation has overtaken you but such as is common to man; and God is faithful, who will not allow you to be tempted beyond what you are able, but with the temptation will provide the way of escape also, that you may be able to endure it." We are to request from God that He will save us from temptation. We must always be on guard and pray to have a heavenly hedge around our daily activities. The reasons we specifically pray for this protection is so our faith will not demise and that our communion with the Lord stays intact. We want to have the courage to say no to all enticements that threaten our spiritual well being.

We pray that God will guard and keep us, that the devil, the world, and our flesh may not deceive us or lead us into misbelief, despair, and other shameful sins. And though we be tempted, we pray that we may still be able to overcome and be victorious.

Trials often present an opportunity to sin. The beginning of this prayer starts with the glorification of God, but it ends with the idea that we are very feeble without Him. If we don't include God as part of our support system we will trip and fall. We aren't capable by ourselves of detouring the forces of evil. We must pray in order to escape these trials. It is during the bad parts of life that often the believer attacks God. Negative circumstances and consequences can undermine our faith.

Often when we aren't suffering we think that we can endure anything thrown to us. Our egos lead us to believe that we will be the next Job of faith. During the rough times we must not become overconfident with our faith. None of us are exempt from bad things happening to us. Even with Emilie's fight with cancer, we are aware that God is teaching something to us and that our faith will become stronger than before. It is through our weaknesses that we become strong.

Some of the great psalms promise that our God is sufficient for all our needs. His strength will lift us up in our times of weaknesses. He is adequate for whatever happens.

Let's not take it for granted when God spares us from many trials of life. Seriously examine each day to see were it not for God's intervention and protection, we would have had trials and distresses in our lives. Little things like not running a red light, not tripping and injuring our body, or not being somewhere where you were scheduled and by that avoiding a tragedy. Be an observer of how God protects you and your family daily. Be earnest in your prayer for protection from evil.

When these trials are permitted in our lives it only means that God has something better for us through these events.

You Are My Hiding Place

O how I love Thy law! It is my meditation all the day.
Thou art my hiding place and my shield;
I wait for Thy Word.

—Psalm 119:97,114

A s a little girl, I loved to play hide-and-seek. After the sun had gone down and it started to get dark, I delighted to find a secret place where no one could find me. When I stayed there, I felt so secure knowing that no one was going to catch me.

As I grew older, I (Emilie) kept looking for such a place where I could get away from all the pressures of life. When I became a Christian and started to have a daily quiet time with my Lord, I was soon aware that my "prayer closet" had become my new hiding place. This was a place where I felt safe from the world, and I could take all the time I needed to read God's Word. At this season of my life, I can afford such luxuries.

My "prayer closet" is an actual place in my home, but I can transport the security to the beach, to a mountain cabin, or to a desert condo. Don't confine your quiet time to just one location. Your hiding place is where you meet God at a regular time each day.

When you feel the stress of the day getting to you, think of the safety you feel in your hiding place. Knowing God is always with you will calm your spirit.

Prayer: Father God, I look so forward to meeting You each day at an appointed time. Your Scriptures still my soul. My anxieties are washed away after our times together. Thank You! Amen.

Action: Create a prayer closet for yourself. If you are lucky enough to have the space, make it pleasant with candles or a soft rug. Let it be a comfort to you.

Today's Wisdom: *"For we have brought nothing into the world, so we cannot take anything out of it either."*

—1 Timothy 6:7

Looking Good

*Arise, shine, for your light has come, and the glory
of the LORD rises upon you....Then you will look and
be radiant, your heart will throb and swell with joy.*

—ISAIAH 60:1,5 NIV

When we arise joyfully, we take action. We get up, make the bed, and start a new day. You have set the tone for the day by deciding to be positive, not negative. You have made a choice that will be beneficial to you. You are literally "looking good."

Be joyful—the Lord has given you the desire to start a new day with a positive attitude. Those around you won't be able to figure out what's happened to you. You are a new person—ready to meet the radiance of the light of the Lord.

There are times when this initial morning joy will be difficult to muster. Your heart might be heavy with an overwhelming list of things to do or your first thoughts might be of your family's many needs. Before you let those pressures determine a negative attitude for the day, face the mirror and smile. It does lift your spirit. Then thank the Lord for the day ahead. Praise Him in advance for all of the blessings you will receive and witness.

Since you are being blessed with a new day, be sure to reflect your joy to the people you meet.

Prayer: Father God, I want my life to be about love, not law; about righteousness, not rules. Show me, this day, what it means to respond to Your Spirit within me. Amen.

Action: Place a picture or a poem by your bedside that makes you immediately smile. Thank the Lord each morning for that particular memory or for the uplifting words.

Today's Wisdom: "Temptation is Satan's opening wedge into a man's being. He does not want to stop there. If a man will obey demonic promptings to do evil, Satan will do worse with him by far than merely to tempt him."

—McCandlish Phillips

He Is Faithful

*You know very well that God's promises
to you have all come true.*

—JOSHUA 23:14 TLB

The statistic in Joshua 23:14 would be like a baseball player getting a hit every time he comes to bat or a quarterback completing every pass he throws. It's an incredible claim that demands focused attention. The odds of this happening are beyond belief, but we know God's promises to be true.

As Joshua is nearing the end of his life, he is giving wisdom to those who will follow him. He is offering nuggets of wisdom before he dies. In his farewell address, Joshua reassures his leaders that they can trust God in all He has promised them. Joshua wants to make sure they don't turn away from their Lord.

I (Emilie) have found this promise to be true in my life. During the last five years, I have held tight to many passages of Scripture that have given me hope as I walked through this valley. God has been faithful to me. He has always followed through on every one of His promises. He can be trusted.

How do you pass along a sense of God's faithfulness to others? It is a remarkable legacy to give your children, friends, coworkers, neighbors, and anyone you encounter. Many people crave evidence of God's love as proof of His promises. By living out your faith, you might be that very bit of evidence someone needs to give his or her life to Christ.

Prayer: Father God, You can be trusted, and I'm going to continue to trust Your promises for my life. I may not always understand them, but I trust You. Amen.

Action: Write down three promises God has fulfilled in your life. Big or small, remembering these kept promises will help you trust Him in all things.

Today's Wisdom: "If the Scriptures say it, I can trust it and claim it for my life."

Near to the Heart of God

Lord, when doubts fill my mind,
when my heart is in turmoil, quiet me and
give me renewed hope and cheer.

—PSALM 94:19 TLB

Life is often filled with unexpected problems and crises. Unrest and despair can darken the way of even the strongest saint. We cannot escape the pressures and dark shadows in our lives, but they can be faced with a spirited strength that our Lord provides.

When Cleland McAfee heard that his two nieces had just died from diphtheria he was stunned. As he turned to Scripture to find some peace through this situation, God gave him the words to this great hymn of the church, "Near to the Heart of God." A choir sang these encouraging words outside the quarantine home of his brother, Howard:

> There is a place of quiet rest, near to the heart of God,
> a place where sin cannot molest, near to the heart of God.
> There is a place of comfort sweet, near to the heart of God,
> a place where we our Savior meet, near to the heart of God.
> There is a place of full release, near to the heart of God,

163

a place where all is joy and peace, near to the heart
of God.

O Jesus, blest Redeemer, sent from the heart of
God,
hold us who wait before Thee near to the heart of
God.

Prayer: *God, may I choose to live courageously regardless
of what may come my way. May I always be sensitive to Your nearness. Amen.*

Action: Read or sing this hymn out loud. It will fill
your heart with the assurance of God's presence.

*Today's
Wisdom:*   *"Keep watching and praying, that you may not
enter into temptation; the spirit is willing, but the
flesh is weak."*

—Matthew 26:41

Give It Away

*It is possible to give away and become richer!
It is also possible to hold on too tightly and
lose everything. Yes, the liberal man shall be rich!
By watering others, he waters himself.*

—PROVERBS 11:24-25 TLB

Western culture says we have to receive first, then we can give. How often does a person spend his or her whole life waiting for someone to give? Love is lost because a partner didn't receive first. The Scripture points out there are two types of people—the givers and the takers.

We've been so blessed in our adult lives because we have been surrounded by givers. We try to stay away from the takers—they strip us of our joy and happiness. Their false expectations leave our lives lacking. The givers give us new hope.

Don't hold on too tightly to the possessions of life. While this is a temptation for many of us, holding on to such things causes us to lose everything, including our Christian perspective. We increase our blessings by giving ourselves away. When we lift others up, we are lifted higher. Whatever God has given to us, we can give to others.

Give your faith, trust, and hope away to those less fortunate.

Prayer: Father God, I place the true riches of my life in Your hands today. All my "first fruits" I give to You. Amen.

Action: Be a giver today. Find a specific way to share of yourself as you interact with others. Make a commitment to show God's faithfulness to another.

Today's Wisdom: "Yet those who wait for the LORD will gain new strength; they will mount up with wings like eagles, they will run and not get tired, they will walk and not become weary."

—Isaiah 40:31

☐ ☐ ☐

Mold Me

*O Lord, you are our Father. We are the clay and you
are the Potter. We are all formed by your hand.*

—Isaiah 64:8 TLB

You would think we would learn this biblical truth early in life, but we usually don't. Sometimes we are slow learners. Occasionally, we have to be hit on the head before we realize what's happening.

In California, we have several artsy communities, such as La Jolla, Laguna Beach, and Carmel. You can observe sculptors or potters work with blocks of clay. We always like to stand for a long time, watching how artists pinch, punch, scrape, dig, and carve these globs of clay. When the clay begins to dry out, the potter will dip his hand into a bucket of water to add moisture to the clay. This water adds life. Then the artist can continue forming the object he wishes to make. The journey continues, and the object begins to take shape. We love to wait long enough to find out what the potter is making. Sometimes we're fooled and the object is much different than both of us had guessed. Even so, as God molds us in His image, we will be amazed at His design.

God is molding something wonderful out of your life. Enjoy the surprises He has planned for you and try not to resist the changes, the transformations, and the new beginnings along the way.

Prayer: Father God, thank You for molding me in Your image. I trust You to continue that process in my life. Amen.

Action: Reflect on your life's journey. Can you think of times when God was shaping you?

Today's Wisdom: "If God is for us, who can be against us?"

—Romans 8:31 NKJV

Love the Brethren

We know that we have passed out of death into life,
because we love the brethren.

—1 JOHN 3:14

o you always pray for others? Probably all of us have, at one time or another, said we would pray but then forgot to do it. Not until I (Emilie) started working with a prayer notebook was I able to write down the names of others that should be upheld in prayer. Before then someone would give me a name to pray for and I would acknowledge it, but I would often get distracted before I could pray for that person.

I realize that I must pray for others because others prayed for me even before I came to know Jesus as Savior and during my lengthy bout with cancer. In Christian kindness I am led to pray for others.

Bob had a faithful Sunday school teacher who challenged him to be a godly young man. Each week she was faithful to prepare her lesson and present it to these young boys. He doesn't even remember her name, but there is one thing he will never forget—she loved those boys in her class. She prayed collectively and individually for that group.

One Easter Sunday she presented the plan of salvation as a lesson, and Bob was so touched that he gave his life to Jesus. During the Sunday morning church service he walked down the aisle to meet the pastor at the front. He expressed his desire to know Jesus as his personal Savior. That evening Bob was baptized. To this day he credits that faithful teacher who prayed for him for helping him make the best decision of his life. This teacher truly loved the brethren.

Prayer: *Father God, what a joy to be able to pray for others. I have witnessed in my life the power of prayer. Without others praying for me I would not be here today. Amen.*

Action: Write down your testimony. Think of who God used in your life to lead you to a real faith. Pray for those people today.

Today's Wisdom: *"Though I fall I will rise; though I dwell in darkness, the LORD is a light for me."*

—Micah 7:8

□ □ □

Walk Firm and Strong

*. . . If you have faith as a mustard seed, you shall say
this to this mountain, "Move from here to there," and
it shall move; and nothing shall be impossible to you.*

—MATTHEW 17:20

If we are praying in God's will, there is nothing too
large for Him. There is no force so big, no energy so
spectacular that it can't be controlled.

If we don't believe our prayer to be effectual, then it
won't be. So much mystery surrounds this word "faith."
Webster defines it as: "Unquestioning belief that does not
require proof or evidence, unquestioning belief in God, a
religion or a system of religious beliefs, anything believed,
complete trust, confidence, or reliance...." Hebrews 11:1
states, "Now faith is the assurance of things hoped for, the
conviction of things not seen."

One thing we do know is that without faith, it is impossible to please God. In our experience, having this kind of
faith means we must not passively sit on the sidelines and
watch others play the game of life. We must be involved. We
must be loving, believing, and caring if we are to use this
transforming power of the Holy Spirit to move our lives forward. We have to be active in the process.

As we look back over our yesterdays, we can see how
our believing in Scripture has gotten us through difficult
financial, physical, mental, and spiritual times. Our enemy

tries to blind us to God's truths. These fears keep us angry and bitter and leave us without peace and power. But with renewed faith, we can know that we are never alone. In Christ, we can have everything we need to be victorious in the battles of life. Sometimes our world falls apart so God can get our attention.

Maybe today you need increased faith so you will be able to get through the difficult season you are in. Ask and it shall be given to you! You must ask.

Prayer: *Father God, my faith is increased when I think about faith. You have given me an abundance of faith, and I am thankful for that. May my faith move mountains. Amen.*

Action: Reflect on your faith. Share what it means to you with someone today.

Today's Wisdom: *"Jabez cried out to the God of Israel, 'Oh, that you would bless me and enlarge my territory! Let your hand be with me, and keep me from harm so that I will be free from pain.' And God granted his request."*

     —*The Prayer of Jabez,* 1 Chronicles 4:10 NIV

Abide in My Love

*"Just as the Father has loved Me,
I have also loved you; abide in My love."*

—John 15:9

If we abide in Christ, we may ask what we will, for we will ask only what the Holy Spirit moves us to ask. We won't have to wonder, but we can ask in a way that is pleasing to God. The Holy Spirit and God the Father are in full agreement about what's best for us.

As Bob and I have grown in our marriage, we have attempted to become one. Our mission statement for this concept has been found in Genesis 2:24, which states, "For this cause a man shall leave his father and his mother, and shall cleave to his wife; and they shall become one flesh."

Sometimes it's scary that we are so much in agreement. At times we catch ourselves finishing each other's thoughts, sentences, and even what we would like to eat for dinner. Some people might consider this boring. We have spent so much time together that his thoughts are my thoughts and his ways are my ways. We love it!

When Jesus challenges us to abide in Him, it's because He knows that the only way we can experience heavenly thoughts is to have heavenly relationships. The best way to know someone is to spend quality time together. As we spend time with our Lord, in essence we spend time with the Trinity—God the Father, God the Son, and God the Holy

Spirit. It is impossible that these three should be at odds with each other. Where your prayer might be directed to one of the Trinity, they each hear and are in agreement to the answer and the proper timing of the answer. Isn't it wonderful that all three in the Trinity so love us that they are informed of what's best for us?

Be assured that as you approach the throne, your requests and petitions have been heard and that the Trinity will send back a response that aligns your prayer with their will for your life.

Prayer: *Father God, we think we can do great things with our technology such as faxes, voice messages, conference calls, cell phones, and so forth, but you and the Trinity could keep track of multiple lines of communication long before e-mail. Amen.*

Action: Approach the throne of the Lord today. Make your requests known.

Today's Wisdom: *"No temptation has overtaken you but such as is common to man; and God is faithful, who will not allow you to be tempted beyond what you are able, but with the temptation will provide the way of escape also, that you may be able to endure it."*

—1 Corinthians 10:13

Abiding Provides Fruit

As the branch cannot bear fruit of itself,
except it abide in the vine; no more
can ye, except ye abide in me.

—JOHN 15:4 KJV

Only as we abide in Christ can we bear fruit. We cannot say to ourselves, "What a fruitful branch I am! Look at me. The vine would not be beautiful without my presence." Without abiding we are no more than the dried-up branches that will be pruned, thrown on a pile, and eventually set on fire or hauled to the landfill.

If our work does not come through Jesus, it counts for nothing—zero. Our fruit producing has to go beyond our natural talent. Each of us has been called for a unique ministry. We need not copy another's ministry because that isn't our calling. Remember, our calling is just for us, and it will not produce fruit if Christ isn't in agreement.

I (Emilie) have had the wonderful opportunity to speak in almost every state of the union plus Canada. Invariably I have women who come up to me and remark, "Someday I want to do just what you are doing." What a wonderful compliment that is to me. We all should think that what we do is the best career that anyone could have. I often remark that they need to be called to do God's work. If He hasn't called you to use your special gifts in this way, you will not be blessed.

Over and over again I am able to witness how God enables people to reap fruit from their gifts. I want women to tell their story, not mine and not yours. God is preparing each of us for our unique ministry. We need to take all the roadblocks that come into our lives and make them freeways to God's truth. We can take every valley and make it a mountaintop experience. Become alert to life; get in the habit of journaling the events of your life. You say you won't forget, but you will. Don't trust your memory, write them down.

God will teach you more in suffering than in victory. Look straight into pain, death, loss of job, a divorce, a hospital stay, and see what God is trying to teach you. Jot down how God is using these difficult times to develop fruit in your Christian walk. Through each valley experience you are gaining information that will use later in life. Each experience will give you an opportunity to bear fruit for our Lord.

Prayer: *Father God, I don't want to bear any fruit on my own. Without your blessing it is nothing but wood, hay, and stubble. Thank You for all the blessings You send me. Amen.*

Action: Start the daily or weekly habit of writing down everything that God is teaching you.

Today's Wisdom: *"Pray that you may not enter into temptation."*
—Luke 22:40

Be Thirsty for Souls

*And there is salvation in no one else; for there is no
other name under heaven that has been given among
men, by which we must be saved.*

—ACTS 4:12

Living in middle-class America, where one's faith is seldom challenged, we can get lulled into complacency and not be thirsty for souls. After all, our first level of friends are mostly believers. We don't hang out with the "real" sinners of life. We're protected from the drunkards, dope dealers, and criminals. Often we're told we live in a very plastic society. And we do! Therefore, sometimes we have to dig deep within to be thirsty for souls. We've had to force ourselves to have actual names of lost individuals on our prayer lists. We just can't write down "pray for the lost"—that's too general in nature. We've got to be specific and identify them by name. These names come from my relatives, neighbors, people I meet, those who sit next to us in church, and fellow employees at the job.

Lord, make us thirsty for those who are lost and have never accepted You as their Savior. We ask ourselves, "Do we really believe there is a hell, separating the lost from God for eternity?" The answer is yes. Even in the good life of America, we must have a passion for those who are lost.

And we must also account daily for our own sins. We must daily go to God, making confession. Individual confession is needed. We have sins you might not realize, but they are there. We all have unexhibited sins in our families, our businesses, and in our private and public lives. Every man and woman has a point of sin wherein we are separated from our fellow sojourners. Each person must make his or her own confession—with full honesty and deep humility. Each must pray, "Search me, O God and know my heart; try me and know my anxious thoughts" (Psalm 139:23). Make me thirsty for my soul and the souls of others who do not know You!

Prayer: *Father God, let me thirst for those who do not know You. Give me joy as I share with others Your gospel. Let me be bold as I proclaim Your message. Amen.*

Action: Pray for someone you know who is not a believer. Commit to praying for him or her regularly.

Today's Wisdom: *"Be careful—watch out for attacks from Satan, your great enemy. He prowls around like a hungry, roaring lion, looking for some victim to tear apart. Stand firm when he attacks. Trust the Lord; and remember that other Christians all around the world are going through these sufferings too."*

—1 Peter 5:8-9 TLB

God Is a God of Love

For God so loved the world, that He gave His only begotten Son, that whoever believes in Him should not perish, but have eternal life.

—JOHN 3:16

f we pray and we do not have love, God will ask, "Why should I hear and answer your prayers? Success will only make you think you can do it on your own." Do we really expect God to bring about answered prayer when the prayer does not include love for God's community? Are we doing that which is pleasing in God's sight? We can't expect a loving God to answer prayers from people who are unloving: after all, God is love.

We are not to run to God morning and night using Him as our protector and as a provider of our needs. We are to *dwell* in God and *live* in Him from sunup to sundown, making God the center of our lives.

With the threat to America by acts of terrorism, we find that our churches take on a whole new meaning of family. Depending upon what section of the country we live in, we readily see that our communities are very multicultured. No longer is America made up of 100-percent European ancestry. We are a country of many sizes, shapes, colors, languages, and religions.

In the years following the explosions of the commercial airlines into the World Trade towers, the Pentagon, and the crashing of a plane in Pennsylvania, we find a great revival taking place in America. Prayers are being conducted in arenas that haven't been the norm and first-time acceptance of Jesus as personal Savior is at an all-time high. Church attendance is up, patriotic songs are being sung throughout the land, people are hugging and crying together, and our divided political parties are focused on the next course of action for our country.

People will be looking to the church for answers to large questions and they will be looking for love. For decades Americans have been looking in all the wrong places for love. With the increased flow of people to our churches, we need to make sure that love is not only found within the walls of our churches, but within our hearts. God has given His love to us; now, in turn, we must give our love to the world.

Prayer: *Father God, where would this world be without Your love? There would be few hospitals, few orphanages, few missions, few churches, few artists, few hymns, and few musicians. The beauty would be lost. Thank You for Your love. Amen.*

Action: Challenge yourself to find one way to give to the world today. Volunteer. Pray for strangers. Serve others.

Today's Wisdom: *"The Lord asks for the whole of your life. Sometimes it feels like a blessed relief, sometimes a painful sacrifice, often a mixture of the two. You give Him all you can of yourself. He fills you with all you could ever want of Him, and then He gives you back yourself as well."*

—Emilie Barnes

For Thine Is the Kingdom, and the Power, and the Glory, Forever. Amen.

A doxology of final thanksgiving

This final doxology found in the King James version was probably not in the original disciples' prayer given by Jesus, but it is appropriate that we end this prayer as it began, with the praising of God, His kingdom, His power, and His glory and a fervent "amen."

This rousing "amen" petitions that all that has been prayed for is acceptable to our Father in heaven, and that it has been heard by Him. For God Himself has commanded us so to pray, and He has promised to hear us. Amen!

This doxology is an affirmation of our trust in God's character and manifests all that has gone before and gives increased hope for the future! This final response is our expression of worship to who God is.

Prayer is something we take with us all day, it is not left behind in our prayer closet. It is our vertical connection with God that gives us the strength and power to live one day at a time. God is listening at our lowest points in life, and He rejoices when we rejoice. Make Him your most personal friend.

Therefore you should say: My prayer is as precious, holy, and pleasing to God as that of St. Paul or of the most holy saint....God does not regard prayer on account of the person, but on account of His words and obedience thereto. For on the commandment on which all the saints rest their prayer I, too, rest mine. Moreover I pray for the same thing for which they all pray and ever have prayed; besides, I have just as great a need of it as those great saints.

—Martin Luther

Study to Show Yourself Approved

For they received the word with
great eagerness, examining the Scriptures daily,
to see whether these things were so.

—ACTS 17:11

According to Martin Luther, "some of his best understandings of Holy Scripture were not so much the result of meditation as they were to prayer." Many students of the Word don't get a full understanding of Scripture until they pray. Then the golden nuggets of the Word are revealed to them. The old maxim, "To have prayed well is to have studied well," is worthy to note. Study and prayer go together. One is meaningless without the other.

Yes, it is true—much study leads to much prayer and much prayer leads to much study. We find it impossible not to have our Bibles with us when we pray or to pray without searching the Scriptures. One leads to the other. Whichever you start with, you will end up with the other.

Psalm 145:18 states, "The LORD is near to all who call upon Him, to all who call upon Him in truth." John 8:32 encourages us to find the truth when it declares, "…You shall know the truth, and the truth shall make you free." In order for us to know truth we must study and pray. Recently we became more aware of the subtleness of evil. It creeps in so easily that we find ourselves overpowered by the mindset of the world. We give a little here and give a little there and pretty soon we are confused and aren't sure what is true. We are continually bombarded by literature, music, the arts, the media to make us lose our focus on truth. After all, we don't want to be labeled a bigot or intolerant.

Romans 12:2 gives us a good warning, "Do not be conformed to this world, but be transformed by the renewing of your mind, that you may prove what the will of God is, that which is good and acceptable and perfect." The only way I know to do this is to study and to pray.

Prayer: *Father God, study for me is such hard work. When I graduated from college, I thought my studying days would be over, but in life I realize we must study if we are to be adequate in our Christian walk. Help me to be faithful in this discipline. Amen.*

Action: Study the Word of God. Hold onto Psalm 145:18 and repeat it to yourself throughout your day.

Today's Wisdom: *"The LORD is good to those who wait for Him, to the person who seeks Him."*

—Lamentations 3:25

□ □ □

The Preciousness of Simplicity

*Therefore I say unto you, What things soever ye
desire, when ye pray, believe that ye receive them,
and ye shall have them.*

—MARK 11:24 KJV

When we go to God in prayer, we go with specifics in mind. When we pray we are to have detailed desires. But prayer should not be a marketing list. Sometimes we may need to make notes to remind us not only of our desires, but also of our adorations, confessions, thanksgivings, and supplications.

Faith is an essential quality of successful prayer. We must truly believe that God really hears and will answer us. Another of today's verse's qualifications is that we believe we receive our desires—not that we might receive, but that we *will* receive. Count your prayer requests as if you have already received them and act as if you have them. There are four qualifications of prayer:

- ❧ There should be definite objects for which to plead
- ❧ We have an earnest desire for its attainment
- ❧ We have a firm faith in God
- ❧ We have an expectation that we will be given what we pray for

Many years ago, we were teaching a "College and Career" Bible study in our home on Sunday evenings. Most of the young adults were college students who had come home for the summer. We had a great time socializing, studying the Bible, and sharing in songs and prayers. One evening the topic was "being specific in our prayers." We just couldn't pray for an apartment, but we had to request location, amount of rent, number of square feet, number of bedrooms, color of paint on the walls, and so on.

In being specific, our assignment was to report back the following week and share how and to what degree our specific prayers were answered. The following Sunday evening as we met in the family room to share, the classmates' mouths were wide open when different young people reported how God answered their specific prayers. One girl had been looking for an apartment with seven qualifications. We couldn't believe it when *all* qualifications were met. You can believe it when we tell you that everyone in that group started praying with specific mentions. Over the course of the summer we had much feedback from those in attendance how being exact helped them give greater meaning to their prayer time. We all learned the preciousness of simplicity. God is so very faithful to those who approach Him with the desires of their hearts.

Prayer: Father God, let me remember to be specific when I pray to You. I don't have to be highbrow or a great orator to have You hear me. Thanks for letting me be simple. Amen.

Action: Pray specific prayers today. Lift up a specific need to the Lord this month. Journal the results.

Today's
Wisdom:

"*Delight yourself in the* LORD; *and He will give you the desires of your heart.*"

—Psalm 37:4

Expect a Blessing

A faithful man will abound with blessings....

—PROVERBS 28:20

hen we pray we are asking for God's glory. We should not be asking for a gift that would glorify us; God is the one to be glorified.

Christmas morning is one of my most favorite mornings of the whole year. I (Emilie) love the excitement of Christmas, the remembrance of the birth of Jesus, our Savior. The carols during the month of December make me think about this small child being born, the innkeeper, the manger, the animals, the angels, the wise men, and the gifts. I love to shop in the busy stores—the people seem especially kind and helpful. I wish we could all be so nice the other 11 months. Even wrapping the presents gives me a thrill for I know that within the box, wrappings, and bows is a gift for that special member of our family I see all year. I've been taking notes from our family members of what they want. Bob wants a new garden rake, Jenny a mixer for the kitchen, Brad a new attaché case, and of course the many wishes of the grandchildren. I just love to give them what they have uttered over the year.

That's the way it is with Jesus. He wants to give us, His loved ones, those prayer requests we have made. Many times we have not because we ask not. We miss blessings because we don't ask for them. As we get to know God more intimately, we need to be sure to let our requests be known.

Prayer: *Father God, throughout Scripture You say You want to bless us, why don't I ask for those blessings You have promised? Give me the courage and bigness of faith to come to You boldly and request those blessings. When I receive them may I always remember to give glory to You! Amen.*

Action: Anticipate a blessing today. Thank the Lord *before* and *after* it takes place.

Today's Wisdom: *"And blessed be His glorious name forever; and may the whole earth be filled with His glory. Amen, and Amen."*

—Psalm 72:19

□ □ □

God's Grace Is Sufficient

The Spirit also helps our weaknesses;
for we do not know how to pray as we should,
but the Spirit Himself intercedes for us
with groanings too deep for words.

—ROMANS 8:26

If I (Emilie) don't have the strength to utter words to heaven with my desires, God's grace will hear my desires without me speaking the words. God understands even our groanings. Our tongues don't have to speak words before He hears them. Parents often know what's in their children's mind without them even talking. Likewise a spouse instantaneously knows what the other is thinking and oftentimes finishes a sentence of the mate. God is like this with us.

The Holy Spirit is the alpha and omega of our prayers. He knows the beginning and the end.

While in the hospital, often I did not know what to pray for. My Bob and I didn't always have the knowledge to properly understand our situation. Oh, yes, we asked questions, but the explanations weren't decoded for our ears. These large multisyllable medical terms were too difficult for our layman ears to grasp. To be honest with you, there were times when we were too tired and stressed to even feel like praying.

However, during these void times, we knew God would redeem our energy, and that He would give us the "right words" for the moment. These were great prayer sessions! We entered with little and exited with joy and satisfaction. How could it be? We were so confused, but God gave us order.

Don't be fearful to pray when you feel the same way we felt. The Holy Spirit will renew your desire for prayer, and He will give you words to speak. God's grace is sufficient for *all* our needs.

Prayer: *Father God, just knowing that You will intercede for me when I don't have the power or words to say is so reassuring. Thanks for knowing me that well. Amen.*

Action: When you pray today, really think about how your words are received and known by God.

Today's Wisdom: *"Never be lacking in zeal, but keep your spiritual fervor, serving the Lord. Be joyful in hope, patient in affliction, faithful in prayer."*

—Romans 12:11-12 NIV

My Lord, Hear Me Now

Be joyful always; pray continually;
give thanks in all circumstances, for this
is God's will for you in Christ Jesus.

—1 Thessalonians 5:16-18 NIV

od gives us the same love as He gives His Son. And since we are children of God, our prayers can't be denied. Since we abide, He listens! Oh, Lord, how we all want this power and confidence in our prayers. We are not to waver in our faith.

What would our churches and families be like if we knew God in such a powerful way? We long to have the mind of God. He is so much greater than we will and can ever be. We realize there are many barriers to our having this kind of power in our prayers. Daily we must break down and eliminate those hindrances from our daily walks with our Lord.

Each of us have different barriers. Whatever they are, we must be willing to come to grips with them and say, "Hindrances, get thee behind me."

Scripture is so very clear that we are to continually abide in Christ if our prayers are to speedily go to the throne for action. As we arise each day and as we recline each evening after a full day, we are to pray with joy rather than looking on prayer as an irksome duty. As we pray with a pure heart and joy, God adds this to us—you shall ask what you will, and it shall be done to you.

Our goal each day is to get to know our Lord better today than we knew Him yesterday. Make it your priority to spend time with God daily. There's not a single right time or correct place; the only requirement is your willing heart.

Prayer:
> *Father God, You truly are a 24/7 God. Thank You for being there when I need You. Thank You for knowing everything I need or desire before I do. My weaknesses glorify Your mighty strength. Amen.*

Action:
> Really express yourself as a child of God. Draw your heavenly Father a picture or sing to Him without reserve.

Today's Wisdom:
> *"God doesn't always smooth the path, but sometimes he puts springs in the wagon."*
>
> —Marshall Lucas

□ □ □

Give Them Away

hen we are given "more and more" of something, we are given an abundance. The dictionary defines "abundance" as having more than enough, having a great supply. Wouldn't life be wonderful if we always had an abundance of those things that make up the good life: health, wealth, success, happiness? A few more cars, a couple of vacation homes, a bigger church budget, another cabinet full of teacups, some more beautiful grandchildren?

The abundance that God has promised us is better than any of those things! He's promised us an abundance of the big three: kindness, peace, and love! If we're living in Him and obeying Him, our lives will overflow with these life-giving qualities. But what if we're feeling shortages of kindness, peace, and love? We can usually look in the mirror to see who's at fault. God gives us what He promises, but we need to live His way. And in order to continue having these qualities in abundance, we must first give them away to others. It's the way God does things: the more we give, the more we get.

Prayer: *Father God, Your majestic love is enough for me today. Help me align my priorities so that they will reflect Your dreams for me. Amen.*

Action: Give away kindness, peace, and love today!

Today's Wisdom: *Lord,*
> *make me an instrument of Your peace,*
> *Where there is hatred, let me sow love;*
> *Where there is injury, pardon;*
> *Where there is doubt, faith;*
> *Where there is despair, hope;*
> *Where there is darkness, light; and*
> *Where there is sadness, joy.*

O divine master,
> *grant that I may not so much*
> *Seek to be consoled as to console;*
> *To be understood as to understand;*
> *To be loved as to love;*
> *For it is in giving that we receive;*
> *It is in pardoning that we are pardoned;*
> *and it is in dying that we are born*
> > *to eternal life.*

—St. Francis of Assisi

Keep Climbing the Mountain

My help is from Jehovah who made the mountains!
And the heavens too!

—PSALM 121:2 TLB

As I (Emilie) have walked through my cancer treatment these last five years, I've often wondered if I am going to make it. Yes, my support group has encouraged me. Hundreds and hundreds of prayer partners have assured me by cards and letters that I am going to make it. My mind, however, is sometimes plagued with negative thoughts about my future. Satan so wants to defeat me by making me lose hope for recovery. Yet my faith remains victorious, and my daily walk with God helps me climb the many mountains put before me.

Bill Martin, Jr. tells a story of how a young Indian boy was able to overcome his fear of failure:

> "Grandfather, will I ever be strong like you?" the little boy asked.
>
> His grandfather reassured him, "You're growing stronger every day."
>
> "How strong must I be, Grandfather?" the boy asked.
>
> "You must be so strong that you will not speak with anger even when your heart is filled with anger. . . . You must be so strong that you will listen to what others are saying even when your

own thoughts are begging for expression. . . . You must be so strong that you will always stop to remember what happened yesterday and foresee what will happen tomorrow so that you will know what to do today."

"Then will I be strong enough to cross over the dark mountains?" the boy asked.

The wise grandfather answered, "You already have crossed some of the dark mountains, my grandson. But these mountains of sorrow have no beginning and no ending. They are all around us. We can only know that we are crossing them when we want to be weak but choose to be strong."

When you're called to cross the dark mountains surrounding you, be brave even when you feel weak. Lift your face skyward and pray that God will give you strength far beyond your expectation.

Prayer: *Father God, today I am weak; I need your strength. Encourage me so I can continue going on. Help me face the unknown, knowing that You know everything. Amen.*

Action: Take one step at a time. Move forward.

Today's Wisdom: *"O my people, trust him all the time. Pour out your longings before him, for he can help!"*

—Psalm 62:8 TLB

You're Uniquely Made

Thank you for making me so wonderfully complex!
It is amazing to think about. Your workmanship
is marvelous—and how well I know it.

—PSALM 139:14 TLB

You're special. In all the world, there's nobody like you. Since the beginning of time there has never been another person like you. Nobody has your smile, your eyes, your nose, your hair, your hands, or your voice. You're special. No one can be found who has your handwriting. Nobody anywhere has your tastes for food, clothing, music, or art. No one sees things just as you do. In all of time there's never been someone who laughs like you and cries like you. And what makes you cry or laugh will never produce identical laughter and tears from anybody else—ever.

You're the only one in all of creation who has your set of abilities.

Oh, there will always be somebody who is better at one of the things you're good at, but no one in the universe can reach the quality of your combination of talents, ideas, abilities, and feelings. Like a room full of musical instruments, some may excel alone, but none can match the symphony sound when all are played together. You're a symphony.

Through all of eternity, no one will ever look, talk, walk, think, or do like you.

Prayer: *Father God, thank You for making me so very special. Give me the desire to be special for you. Amen.*

Action: Do something today that shows you are a special person.

Today's Wisdom: *"You're special...you're rare. And in all rarity there is great value. Because of your great value, you need not attempt to imitate others...you will accept—yes, celebrate your differences.*

"You're beginning to see that God made you special for a purpose.

"He must have a job for you that no one else can do as well as you.

"Out of the billions of applicants, only one is qualified, only one has the right combination of what it takes.

"That one is you, because...you're special."

—Reta Crane

Touch the Stars

*Forgetting the past and looking forward to what lies
ahead, I strain to reach the end of the race and receive
the prize for which God is calling us up to heaven
because of what Christ Jesus did for us.*

—PHILIPPIANS 3:13-14 TLB

Stars have too long been symbols of the unattainable. They should not be so. For although our physical hands cannot reach them, we can touch them in other ways. Let stars stand for those things which are ideal and radiant in life; if we seek sincerely and strive hard enough, it is not impossible to reach them, even though the goals seem distant at the onset. And how often do we touch stars when we find them close by in the shining lives of great souls, in the sparkling universe of humanity around us? (Esther Baldwin York).

Have you ever considered that you are a star people can touch? Does your life light up the room when you enter? You can become a star in so many areas of life if you will forget the past and look forward to what lies ahead. All of the great conquests of life have started as a little idea in someone's head. It's what is done with the idea that counts.

What are your deepest dreams? Reach out today and plan how you are going to turn those thoughts into reality. Don't let them fall to the ground and perish. Nurture and water them until sunlight makes them grow. Aim high!

Prayer: *Father God, I love to look into the vastness of space to see the twinkle of Your stars. May I be able to reach out and touch their light. Amen.*

Action: Dream big dreams, and act upon them.

Today's Wisdom: *"I thank You, my Creator and Lord, that You have given me these joys in Your creation, this ecstasy over the works of Your hands. I have made known the glory of Your works to men as far as my finite spirit was able to comprehend Your infinity. If I have said anything wholly unworthy of You, or have aspired after my own glory, graciously forgive me. Amen."*

—Johannes Kepler

Give Prayer a Try

*Because he bends down and listens,
I will pray as long as I breathe!*

—PSALM 116:2 TLB

Who has time to pray? My 'To Do' list is always longer than my day. I run from the time the alarm goes off in the morning until I fall into bed at night. How can I possibly find time to do one more thing? When could I find even a few minutes to read the Bible or pray?"

I felt that way for many years, but finally I decided to make prayer one of my top priorities. I decided to get up 30 minutes before the rest of the family. The days that I did this went so much smoother. I had more control of the day, and my emotional stability was much more even. I'm glad I established this habit in my life because when I faced dark times, I already had a line of communication with my heavenly Father. We had already become prayer partners together. Are you wondering what to talk to God about when you pray? Here are a few suggestions.

    ⊳ Praise God for who He is—the Creator and Sustainer of the whole universe, who is interested in each of us (Psalm 150; Matthew 10:30).

❧ Thank God for what He has done for you, for all He is doing for you, and for all that He will do for you (Philippians 4:6).

❧ Confess your sins. Tell God about the things you have done and said and thought for which you are sorry. He tells us in 1 John 1:9 that He is "faithful and righteous to forgive us our sins."

❧ Pray for your family and for friends or neighbors who have needs—physical and spiritual. Ask God to work in the heart of someone you hope will come to know Jesus as Savior. Pray for your government officials, for your minister, and for missionaries and other Christian servants (Philippians 2:4).

❧ Pray, too, for yourself. Ask for guidance for the day ahead. Ask God to help you do His will, and ask Him to arrange opportunities to serve Him throughout the day (Hebrews 10:36).

Prayer: *Father God, may I never forget to call on You in every situation. Amen.*

Action: Decide today that you will give prayer a try. See what talking to God can do.

Today's Wisdom: *"How can I help but rejoice when I'm reminded that I serve a living God and that He will endure forever."*

—Emilie Barnes

Don't Be Afraid to Look Back

This is My body, which is given for you;
do this in remembrance of Me.

—LUKE 22:19

In the last few months of her life, humorist Erma Bombeck wrote one of her most moving columns. In it, she shared what she would do differently if she could live her life over again. She would have appreciated the little things in life a lot more and had less regrets. In the end, she was looking back on life and remembering all the little phases and events we all often overlook the first time around.

When we take communion at our church, the elements are placed on a table with these words carved on the front of the table, "This Do in Remembrance of Me." The Scriptures state very clearly that we are to look to the cross and remember what Jesus did there for us.

As we review our lives, let's make sure we have accepted that Jesus suffered for us and our sins on the cross and paid the price for our redemption with His death because of His tremendous love for us. As we look back, may we clearly remember the cross, the bread, and the cup of wine.

When we look back on these things with confidence in the Lord, we are able to look ahead with assurance to His kingdom—and it is such a beautiful sight.

Prayer: *Father God, I remember when I accepted Jesus as my personal Savior. What a wonderful memory! May I reflect on this decision with great gladness because it was the day that I saw the beauty of my future with You, Lord. Amen.*

Action: Write in your journal your recollection of when you became a child of God. Include date, time, place, and situation.

Today's Wisdom: *"Let endurance have its perfect result, that you may be perfect and complete, lacking in nothing."*

—James 1:4

So Let It Grow

Is your life full of difficulties and temptations?
Then be happy, for when the way is rough,
your patience has a chance to grow.

—JAMES 1:2-3 TLB

hroughout Scripture, we read of victory over troubles and suffering. Helmut Thielicke, a great German pastor and theologian, testified to this kind of victory during the horrors of World War II.

"We live by God's surprises," he proclaimed after he had personally suffered under the Nazis. As a pastor, he wrote to young soldiers about to die; he comforted mothers, fathers, and children after the bombs killed their loved ones. He preached magnificent sermons week after week as bombs blew apart his church and the lives and dreams of his parishioners. He spoke of God not only looking in love at His suffering people, weeping with them as they were surrounded by flames, but of God's hand reaching into the flames to help them, His own hand scorched by the fires.

From the depths of suffering and the wanton destruction caused by the Nazi regime, Thielicke held out a powerful Christian hope. To Germans disillusioned by the easily manipulated faith of their fathers, he quoted philosopher Peter Wust: "The great things happen to those who pray. But we learn to pray best in suffering."

Prayer, suffering, joy, and the surprises of God...they are all tightly enmeshed. But many people shrink from suffering, afraid that it will kill their joy and keep them from experiencing "great things." When we are rightly related to God, life is full of joyful uncertainty and expectancy. We do not know what God is going to do next; He packs our lives with surprises all the time. Prayer becomes the lens through which we begin to see from God's perspective.

Prayer: *Father God, I want to live life in expectation of your surprises. I want to stand on tiptoe to see Your mysteries unveiled for me. Amen.*

Action: Stand on your tiptoes to see what God is going to do next in your life.

Today's Wisdom: *When our vision is*
Clouded by circumstance...
God sees clearly.
When our understanding is
Shadowed by questions...
God knows perfectly.
When our path is
Shaded with uncertainty...
God leads faithfully.

—Author unknown

☐ ☐ ☐

Thank You

Lately I (Emilie) have spent a lot of time waiting in the reception areas of doctors' offices. During all this waiting, I have the opportunity to talk to people who have been diagnosed with a disease that will shorten their life expectancies—they have received the bad news. I have become aware that I no longer want to wait for bad news before I begin to appreciate life.

I've always been a thankful person, giving gratitude to God for what He has given me, but now I'm more dedicated to not taking for granted one single day of my existence because life can be very short.

Our situation can change at the drop of a hat. Bad news can come in a moment's notice. We have no promise that we will live forever; in fact, "it is appointed for men to die" (Hebrews 9:27). As I look around today, I can truly thank God abundantly for the simple things of life—sleeping, walking, running, heartbeats, husband, children, peace— things I used to take for granted. I find myself pausing several times a day to thank God for all my blessings.

Prayer: Father God, I don't want to wait to receive bad news before I thank You. You are the Giver of all goodness. Thank You! Amen.

Action: Take time to thank God for all your blessings.

Today's Wisdom: "So be glad—yes, actually be glad that you have problems. Be grateful for them as implying that God has confidence in your ability to handle these problems with which He has entrusted you. Adopt this attitude toward problems, and it will tend to siphon off the depression you may have developed from negative reactions to them. And as you develop the habit of thinking in hopeful terms about your problems, you will find yourself doing much better with them."

—Norman Vincent Peale

Take Stock and Take Heart

*Commit your work to the Lord,
then it will succeed.*

—Proverbs 16:3 TLB

When was the last time you did something just for you? We all need periods of reappraisal and renewal—time to take stock and take heart. A quiet time gives us the opportunity to identify our most cherished goals and develop ways to achieve them. It also contributes to a sense of inner peace and makes us feel more in control of life.

How do you get started with a quiet time? Let me suggest some tools to help you. The first one is the Bible. Read it daily and say your prayers. Another helpful tool is to record your prayers, thoughts, and feelings in a journal.

Listen to uplifting music while you write. Take this opportunity to turn off the TV. God wants to speak to our hearts when things are quiet around us.

Read a good Christian book. Schedule activity dates for yourself, and pencil them on your calendar. Make sure you keep these dates.

Our crowded schedules and noisy world can make it difficult to take stock or take heart. And what do you do about the guilt of taking time for yourself? Get over it!

Prayer: *Father God, I want to think about You today. I want to bask in Your love and feel Your acceptance all around me. Amen.*

Action: Relax. Sit on the porch. Enjoy an afternoon reading a book. Make moments just for you.

Today's Wisdom: *"Taste and see that the LORD is good; blessed is the man who takes refuge in him."*

—Psalm 34:8 NIV

God Hears Our Prayers

*And we are sure of this, that he will listen to us
whenever we ask him for anything in line with his
will. And if we really know he is listening when we
talk to him and make our requests, then we can be
sure that he will answer us.*

—1 John 5:14-15 TLB

This passage caused me concern because I prayed for complete healing but was disappointed. I wasn't getting better. Every day—sometimes many times during the day—my Bob and I prayed fervently that I wouldn't have to go through all that goes with cancer. We prayed like Jesus: "Lord, take this cup from me. Spare me from all the chemo, radiation, doctors, hospitals, needles, nurses, CAT scans, lung X-rays, dehydration…."

You know the feeling when a friend doesn't do what you expect. See, in today's verse all I read was, "Make your requests known; then we can be sure that he will answer us." Not until I had read, prayed, and meditated on this promise, did I find the clincher midway through this passage: "whenever we ask him for anything in line with his will."

One of the great lessons I have learned is to seek God's will for my life. I can't stress enough how much more effective your prayer life will be when you realize that God has a plan for each of our lives. You begin to look at life very differently. Trials, joys, and learning experiences can be viewed through God's eyes. All of a sudden the twists and turns you have maneuvered are placed in the context of a map of your life's journey.

Prayer: *Father God, help me seek Your will for my life. Let me be at peace with Your plan and timetable. From experience, I know I can trust You with everything. Amen.*

Action: Evaluate your prayers to see if they fit in with God's will for your life. Are you selfishly seeking your own will?

Today's Wisdom: *"Prayer has never been a mail-order business for me; a place where I get what I order when I want it. It is a communication level with God and those who share in the love of God so that we may understand His will and act upon it as it is made clear to us."*

—James Chapman

He Made Us

*The Lord is God! He made us—we are
his people, the sheep of his pasture.*

—PSALM 100:3 TLB

We live in such a hurry-up world. Each year the pace of living seems to double. We want faster cars, microwaves, faxes, and Internet. We can't stand having to wait for anything. People even complain how long it takes to get fast food. What takes so long? Hurry, hurry—please hurry.

Sometimes that's also the way we look upon God as He molds us in His image. His timetable seems so slow; we want to be mature Christians now, not 15 or 20 years from now.

When my doctor told me I had cancer, I thought I would be cured in about six months. Never did I expect the process to last for five years (and counting). When my medical team told me I would be in Seattle for at least a hundred days, my first thought was, *Why so long? Can't they go faster?*

God doesn't operate in a hurry-up fashion. His schooling takes more time than we expect it to. Learn to slow down and relax; learn to be still and appreciate the solitude of this period of your life. You are being hand-tooled by God—don't rush Him. He is designing a masterpiece.

Prayer:

Father God, teach me to slow down. I get in such a hurry. Let me live on Your timetable and not by my watch. Help me to embrace the moments that are meant to strengthen me, renew me, and to bring my thoughts back to You. Amen.

Action:

Slow down and allow God to take His time with His masterpiece.

Today's Wisdom:

"The night is given us to take breath, to pray, to drink deeply at the fountain of power. The day, to use the strength which has been given us, to go forth to work with it till the evening."

—Florence Nightingale

One Day at a Time

*You saw me before I was born and scheduled
each day of my life before I began to breathe.
Every day was recorded in your book!*

—Psalm 139:16 TLB

God, who loves us, numbers our days—but we don't know how many we will have. God, who loves us, will direct our paths—but we don't know where they will take us or what we will discover along the way.

Any number of things could happen tomorrow. An illness. An accident. A financial reversal. Death. And though none of these disasters can separate you from Christ, they can still change everything about your life. They can rob you of precious time. They can take away from the time you have to spend with loved ones or embrace the gifts and talents you possess. So live fully now!

Take soup to your neighbors or point out the stars to your children. Feed the hungry, visit the sick, and share the Good News of Christ.

God has given you the gift of this moment, this day—it's full of blessings and opportunities. Gifts are made to be used, not just stored on a shelf. So tear off the wrapping, pull apart the tissue paper, and say yes to whatever you find.

Most of all, say yes to the Lord, who loves you. Give Him back the gift of your hours and your days.

Prayer: *Father God, I know my days are numbered, and you know how many it will be. I want to live each day as if it were my last. Thank You for each day. Amen.*

Action: As You rise this morning, decide how you want to express God's love. Make today count.

Today's Wisdom: *"Have Thine own way, Lord,*
Have Thine own way.
Thou art the Potter,
I am the clay."

—Adelaide A. Pollard

Notes

1. Taken from Emilie Barnes, *15 Minutes of Peace with God* (Eugene, OR: Harvest House Publishers, 1997), pp. 88-90.

2. Taken from Bob Barnes, *Minute Meditations™ for Men* (Eugene, OR: Harvest House Publishers, 1998), p. 43.

3. Ibid., pp. 137-38.

4. Taken from Bob Barnes, *15 Minutes Alone with God for Men* (Eugene, OR: Harvest House Publishers, 1995), pp. 189-90.

5. Taken from Emilie Barnes, *15 Minutes of Peace with God,* pp. 114-17.

6. Taken from Emilie Barnes, *15 Minutes Alone with God* (Eugene, OR: Harvest House Publishers, 1995), pp. 66-68.

Other Minute Meditations™ Books
by Bob & Emilie Barnes

Minute Meditations™ for Busy Moms
Emilie Barnes
Time-challenged moms get encouragement and direction for reflecting Christ in their homes and beyond. Short prayers and action steps help you put challenging notions into motion. A prayerful pick-me-up for mothers on the go.

Minute Meditations™ for Couples
Bob & Emilie Barnes
Giving you quick opportunities to draw near to God—and each other—these inspiring quotes, encouraging words, and practical advice reflect the deep bonds trials spark in couples committed to each other.

Minute Meditations™ for Healing and Hope
Emilie Barnes
The hope of the Lord is yours. These devotions, written while Emilie was undergoing cancer treatment, reflect the emotional needs and dependence on God that adversity builds in people. Emilie and Bob offer encouragement and advice for anyone experiencing turbulent times.

Minute Meditations™ for Men
Bob Barnes
Is finding meaningful time with God possible with all the demands on your time? Yes. These two- and three-minute meditations, packed with encouragement, will make an incredible difference in how you handle the day's pressures and maximize your time with God.

Minute Meditations™ for Women
Emilie Barnes
Encouraging you to seek the Lord in every circumstance, these five-minute readings offer gentle insights and Scripture to highlight the joys of sharing Jesus, encouraging husbands, becoming children of God, and more.

Other Harvest House Books
by Emilie Barnes